Wonderful Wimbledon

Wonderful Wimbledon

ALASTAIR REVIE

PELHAM BOOKS

First published in Great Britain in 1972 by Pelham Books Ltd
52 Bedford Square, London, W.C.1
1972

7207 0555 X

Set and printed in Great Britain by
Tonbridge Printers Ltd Peach Hall Works, Tonbridge, Kent
in Garamond, eleven on twelve point on paper supplied by
P. F. Bingham Ltd, and bound by James Burn
at Esher, Surrey

Contents

Illustrations

Chapter One / The Honour and the Corn

Top people have played lawn tennis at Wimbledon since 1875 – only shortly after the game was invented. Once upon a time they were exclusively people of previlege and tournament competitors even included a future king of England. More recently they have embraced the entire host of tennis's glamorous superstars, who are today's top people.

No other game has an international centre to compare with Wimbledon. It is Mecca for the tennis faithful throughout the world, and not even St Andrews has the same pull for modern golfers. Wimbledon, too, has uniquely and subtly kept up with and even ahead of the times. Its titles are the most treasured in the game. In addition to being the oldest of all the international championships, the Wimbledon Fortnight is the most reported, talked about and televised championship in the world.

The 500 best players in the game annually send in an entry form for Wimbledon. Some are accepted automatically, because their records justify it. Others have to enter a qualifying competition, which is generally regarded by all concerned as one of the most poignantly harrowing weeks of the tennis year. The result is that every June the world's top 128 men and 96 women in lawn tennis deem it an honour to find themselves invited to participate in the Wimbledon singles by the strict organisers – a joint committee of the All-England Club and the Lawn Tennis Association.

To achieve the esteem of a head-to-head, monarch-of-the-glen battle on the Centre Court is every dedicated player's aim; while to win a Wimbledon singles' title is the accolade than which none is greater. As Rod Laver has put it, recalling how he felt in 1968 when Wimbledon went 'open': 'Future players will never know the elation of being recognised as respectable men again.' And, as he added when he won the first Open Wimbledon: 'What is there left to prove?'

Longsightedly, a handful of young croquet enthusiasts had foreseen Wimbledon's tennis potential some 100 years before, and had first cashed in on it. Topsy-like, the game of lawn tennis had begun to grow, in the late 'sixties and early 'seventies of the nineteenth century, as a desired alternative to the established games of real tennis and rackets. There had been no one inventor, although it has to be said that all the main claimants were English, and that most of them were, for no recognisable reason, retired army officers.

Prominent among the pioneers were two cricketing stalwarts, Major T. H. Gem and Captain J. B. Periera, who introduced a form of tennis to the lawns of their club at Edgbaston, Birmingham, in 1868. Thereafter various versions were played at other cricket clubs in England and Wales, in an indolent sort of way, until, in 1873, a Major (retired) Walter Wingfield, a forty-year-old puzzle compiler and occasional inventor, patented his version under the curious name of 'Sphairistike'. Commercially inclined, Major Wingfield went out on the road and sold the necessary equipment to various interested parties.

In addition to charging six guineas for a package which included one net, two rackets, twelve balls and a book of rules, the Major sold extra rackets at a pound a time and balls at five shillings a dozen. Gallantly but inconsistently, he reduced the price of rackets to ladies (same size and weight) by five bob, but respectfully asked them to pay full price for the tennis balls – 'rubber cored and flannel covered'. He humbly admitted, placing a guarded finger to his lips to command silence, that among his honoured customers were 'royalty and most ranks of the aristocracy'. And he was at pains to point out that the game of sphairistike had been evolved only after years of research into indoor racket-and-ball games played in ancient Greece and in Elizabethan England.

He had taken the name from the Greek and had designated the playing area a 'court' in deference to Henry VIII, who had been 'an accomplished performer'.

Major Wingfield was ever solicitous towards the women, who

he hoped would take up sphairistike in equal numbers to men. But in the main the Press was against him on this score. It was generally considered to be far too energetic a game for genteel Victorian ladies. 'The voluminous skirts worn today make it totally out of order to play racquet games of this type,' one female writer opined. And a letter to *The Times* said: 'Anyone playing in partnership with a lady should be ready for certain eventualities. One of these is that the lady will invariably be nonplussed by the drop stroke, and her partner must always be prepared to run for these shots, as on him will rest the responsibility of returning them . . .'

One of the truly original features of sphairistike was an hour-glass shaped court, produced by making the net narrower than the baselines, and by curving the sidelines so that short, angled shots were virtually impossible. The Major also made provision for mixed doubles in the rules, and for ladies serving from a point nearer the net than the 'diamond' from which gentlemen would serve.

However, among the Major's serious mistakes was to make no allowance for double faults, there being no limit to the number of serves allowed to each player; inevitably this resulted in much frustrated boredom, especially when inexperienced ladies were learning the game. Another error was that the service courts, into which the server delivered his underarm shots, abutted the baseline instead of the net. Only the servers could score a point, and if they lost the rally the service changed sides. The fifteen points that made up each game were known as 'aces'.

In due course, Major Wingfield was persuaded by customers (who had been varying the rules and even the size of the court or the height of the net as they thought fit) to modify his game and, in particular response to their demands, he straightened the sidelines of his court, while retaining the hourglass effect. Each half of the playing area then measured 13 yards at the baseline, 7 yards at the net, and 14 yards at the sidelines. At about this time, two years after he had patented sphairistike (or lawn tennis as he was now calling it) the Major began to use his army connections to get the game going overseas.

One of the first far-flung units to try out his ideas and equipment was the British garrison in Bermuda, and it happened that, in 1874, tennis was being played on the lawns of the officers' mess there when a wealthy American spinster, Miss Outerbridge, chanced by. In no time she had obtained the major's address and later in the same year she preened herself on seeing lawn tennis being played for the first time in the United States, at Camp Washington. Abroad, as in England, it was as a snobbish social 'plus' that the new game was spreading from lawn to lawn.

Meanwhile, in response to competitive experience, further demands were being made for Wingfield's wayward rules to be tidied up and embodied in a code which could be sealed with the approval of some respected official body or other. Not too surprisingly, approaches were made to the pundits of the Marylebone Cricket Club, who had long urged Britain and its Empire to 'play up, play up and play the game', and they loftily agreed to give guidance and advice.

The M.C.C. Tennis and Racquets Sub-committee, set up to do the job, called together as many interested parties as it was able to locate, ruminated on a vast accumulation of suggestions, including some of great eccentricity, and issued, in 1875, 'The Original Standardised Rules of Lawn Tennis'. These were far from perfect. The language was unclear in many paragraphs, as was apparently the intent. Wingfield's hour-glass court was perpetuated, albeit with the 'waist' thickened to 8 yards. Net heights were still 5 feet at the posts, but were reduced to 4 feet at the centre. Scoring was to be by 'hand-in' and 'hand-out', as in rackets', with the hand-in side alone allowed to serve and score. Only one service fault was to be permitted in future, and it was deemed better that the service should land between the net and the service line, rather than between service line and baseline. The balls were to be $2\frac{1}{4}$ inches in diameter and $1\frac{1}{2}$ ounces in weight. Despite criticisms, the M.C.C.'s imperfect rules were followed fairly faithfully for a couple of years, and might have continued to hold back the game for much longer but for the developments at Wimbledon.

It was certainly not by chance that, at about this stage, Wimbledon's All-England Club got its strong hands on the new baby and proceeded to burp it into shape. Their paternal move came about in this way: The All-England Croquet Club had been founded in 1869 by a number of well-born young men who lived in London and desired a nearby location where they could indulge daily their passion for croquet. Having contributed to a kitty of about £600, they cast around for a suitable site for their enterprise. Wimbledon seemed ideal. A quiet but historically-important and attractively-landscaped suburb, to the south-west of London, it boasted the motto *sine labe decus* (usually translated as 'honour without stain') and was suitably snooty... although it is perhaps not inappropriate to note with hindsight that Wimbledon's crest has its corny aspect, in the form of a large sheaf atop the entire device.

The half-dozen doughty young men contrived to find four acres of grassland, in Worple Road, Wimbledon, which they could rent at little more than £50 per year. Soon they had it laid out as a number of croquet lawns flanking a comfortable club-house, at a total cost of about £450.

At once, the club secretary set the tone. 'Gentlemen,' read the first notice on the board outside his office, 'are requested not to play in their shirt-sleeves when ladies are present'. Thick flannel blazers may not have been the ideal dress for croquet on a warm summer day, but, dammit, appearances were important, and clothes made the gentleman!

The All-England Croquet Club having prospered and brought forth membership abundantly for six years, it was scarcely surprising that one of the go-ahead young founders should propose to the committee early in 1875 that part of their now-lush turf should be set aside for the purposes of playing lawn tennis and badminton. This was readily agreed, and the treasurer prudently set aside £25 to purchase the necessary equipment. As lawn tennis was a more energetic game than croquet, it was also considered important to provide anti-B.O. bathing facilities... and before long dressing-rooms, too, had to be added.

So successful were these innovations that within two years the tennis membership of what was now known as the All-England Croquet and Lawn Tennis Club had greatly exceeded that established for croquet, and there was now no doubt in the committee members' minds where future riches lay. Nor were they lacking in the stature necessary to follow through on their successful enterprise. In early 1877, they adopted the Rules of Lawn Tennis, as published by the M.C.C., and co-opted two 'experts' on to their committee. Immediately after these changes had taken place, it was unanimously agreed, at a specially-convened spring meeting of the club, that the world's first lawn tennis tournament should be launched at Wimbledon with all speed.

The event was scheduled to run for a fortnight from Monday, 9 July, 1877, with the fascinating social proviso that it had to be suspended for two days in the middle week-end to allow members to attend the Eton v. Harrow cricket match at Lords. It was also decided that the tournament provided an excellent excuse to alter the M.C.C. rules, which had been proving almost unworkable, and a committee was set up to do so. It consisted of All-England founder, Henry Jones, ex-M.C.C. expert Julian Marshall, and real tennis star C. G. Heathcote.

They proved to be three wise men, with a vengeance, inasmuch as their rules – which differed fundamentally and extensively from those issued by the M.C.C. – have remained intact, save for a few minor details, for almost 100 years. On such splendidly far-sighted visions was the magic of the early Wimbledon created and the foundations of today's successes laid.

In preparing the new rules, the first thing the All-England committee did was to excise most of the remaining ideas propagated by Major Wingfield. Not only was he not pleased to be ignored; be bombarded the three men with further eccentric schemes he felt should be added to the rule book. One of these was that the outdoor tennis season could be extended if nets were erected on suitable ponds and if the players merely exchanged plimsolls for boots and skates!

The hour-glass court, with its ladylike waist, was abandoned for ever. The court to be prepared for the first Wimbledon championships was to be a rectangular one, measuring 26 yards by 9, with a net (39 inches high at the middle) fixed to 5-foot high posts, erected 3 feet outside the court. The balls were to be covered with white flannel. The game of 15 aces (taken from the system used in rackets) was considered slow and clumsy; scoring as we know it today was devised and introduced. In future, the service was to be made with one foot behind the baseline, and one service fault was to be allowed without penalty. A ball falling on the line was to be good, and so were all net-cords. Players were to change ends after each set.

Mr Henry Jones took it upon himself to referee the first championship, 'open to all amateurs', for which a silver challenge cup (value twenty-five guineas) had been offered by the proprietors of *The Field,* the principal sporting magazine of the day. The other prizes were to be a twelve-guinea Gold Champion prize for the winner; a Silver Champion seven-guinea prize for the runner-up; and a third prize, value three guineas.

The balls laid on for the tournament had been specially moulded for the occasion and their white covers had been tightly hand-sewn over the rubber. Excellent though they were for general play, it was found on testing that no two balls were the same in terms of hardness or bounce, so that, when this news leaked out, much sleight of hand in ball selection was employed by the semi-professional real tennis and rackets players who dominated the lists.

The tennis rackets in use were mainly pear-shaped ones adapted from those long employed in real tennis. Costing up to two guineas each, their frames were constructed of well-seasoned rent ash, and their gut strings tended to be coarse and rather slack. In weight, they could be several times heavier than the average racket today. Then, as is indeed the case still in the 'enlightened' 1970s, there was no rule limiting the size, weight, or method of manufacture of a tennis racket.

Shades of recent scoring innovations, too – the referee at the first Wimbledon tourney chose to cut short matches that looked like going on and on by calling 'sudden death' after five-all!

Overhead service had not been thought of in 1877, and even delivery from the shoulder was considered to be difficult and dangerous. Most players served underhand, using plenty of cut in place of power. And the twenty-two players who took part in the first Wimbledon tournament confessed to be much confused by the scoring and grateful for Mr Jones's obvious mastery over it.

Players wagered on themselves or against each other, and odds were offered in the crowd for and against this and that favourite as the matches proceeded. In the event, the first Wimbledon singles' title was won by an 'outsider', by means of gamesmanship. Mr Spencer W. Gore, a racket player (and an old-Harrovian) rumbled the fact that the steeply-dipping net could be used time after time to win matches. Against each opponent, he advanced to the net at the earliest possible moment and thence launched sustained volleying attacks, secure in the knowledge that he was protected from passing shots by the 5-foot height of the net at the posts. The fact that he was a big man with long arms and legs certainly did not work against him in these enterprises.

It was the first time, as far as is known, that volleying had ever been introduced scientifically into any ball game; the 'net' result was that Mr Gore marched straight through to the final and defeated Mr W. C. Marshall therein, at 4.30 p.m. on the afternoon on Thursday, 19 July, before any competitor had figured out an answer to his volleying technique.

Attendances had been fairly good during the two weeks of sporadic matches, and 200 enthusiasts paid one shilling each to see the final. This may not seem a great achievement in the light of today's prices and attendances, but it left the All-England Committee members well pleased with the fruits of their pioneer effort, which included a profit of nearly eleven pounds over the fortnight, comparing most favourably with an average of seven shillings profit from the annual croquet championships. Wimbledon had staked its claim to tennis leadership just in time. Overseas clubs would soon be flexing their muscles and shouting the odds.

Indeed, the world's first national lawn tennis association was founded in the United States within four years of Wimbledon's first tournament, and fielded the first U.S. championships in the same year, 1881 – albeit using the Wimbledon rule book and English-made balls.

Three years earlier, in 1878, the game had been formally introduced to Australia, when a court had been prepared at the Melbourne Cricket Club; but the first tournament in the southern hemisphere, the 1880 Victoria Championships, had been organised on a regional rather than a national basis.

Elsewhere, the sporting leaders of many countries with British affinities were awakening to the possibilities of lawn tennis. In 1875, it had caught on in clubs and messes throughout India; and in the same year, the Rio de Janeiro Cricket Club had launched the game in Brazil.

Europe had been relatively slow to catch on. The game was spread eventually by the English, first via the Channel holiday resorts of France, from 1877. It was not until 1883 that the first three courts were laid out in Hamburg, and the first championships were not held there until 1887. Then everything snowballed, and within a decade lawn tennis was well established in

Italy, Switzerland, Scandinavia, Hungary, Finland, the Near East, the Middle East, Argentina, Jamaica, Colombia and South Africa.

Meanwhile, a fresh look had been taken at the rules, in the light of Spencer Gore's volleying tactics. Before the second Wimbledon fortnight, it was decided to lower the net a few inches (partly as a result of which Spencer Gore was defeated 7–5, 6–1, 9–7 by fellow-Harrovian P. F. Hadow, the other part of Hadow's success being that he instinctively invented the lob in response to Gore's volleys) and in 1880 it was lowered again at the posts to 4 feet. The service line was also brought in to a distance of 7 yards from the net. In the same year, the hand-stitched ball disappeared in favour of an Ayres ball, of known standard weight and size, and admission prices to Wimbledon's 12 courts in use in the Championships was increased to half-a-crown. A new lease had been signed for 12 years early in 1880, allowing extra stands and dressing-room accommodation to be added, and the entries that year rose to 60.

In 1882, the net height was finally fixed at today's standard of 3 feet in the centre and 42 inches at the posts. The game had now become so popular that the profits from the championships had risen from £100 in 1879 to an average of over £500, and the overall profits from the club were of the order of £800. The improved dressing-room facilities had led to escalating membership on the tennis side until, at the 1883 Annual General Meeting, the name of Croquet was expunged from the club's title. (It was, however, put back twenty years later in the second-billing position, as the All-England Lawn Tennis and Croquet Club – this in memory of the game which got the club going but, alas, is no longer played there).

The year 1883 was an important one for Wimbledon, when the club played host to its first American law tennis visitors, Messrs. C. M. and J. S. Clark, who watched the tournament and took back some of its innovations to the States, including a detailed score-board which had been erected for the championships.

By this time, Wimbledon had also found its first star player. Gore and Hadow had been followed, in 1879, by an unknown from Yorkshire, a young cleric, J. T. Hartley, who was so unprepared for his success that he had to dash back home in the middle of the tournament to deliver a sermon and rearrange some of his parish duties. He had overcome his surprise to repeat his success in 1880, but lawn tennis was changing and the first of the dedicated young men of tennis (practising several hours a day) swept the board in 1881 and defeated Hartley ignominiously in the final, with a score-line of 6–0, 6–2, 6–1. He was 20-year-old William Renshaw, and he was to reign at Wimbledon for six splendid years. Indeed between 1881 and 1889, he was to establish a record, which looks like standing for ever, of seven Wimbledon singles' titles, including six in a row. Another unique aspect of this championship run was that, in two successive finals, William Renshaw was opposed by and defeated his equally-handsome twin brother, Ernest. And in 1888, twin Ernest became the first-ever All-Comers' Singles champion, when he defeated another star of the time, H. F. Lawford, the man who had broken William's run of successes in 1887.

Lawford had been elected to the All-England Club committee a few years before and was proving an admirable administrator of great common sense and integrity – a splendid addition to the assorted wise men already in residence. Together with Henry Jones (who had now opened up as an eccentric – 'a familiar figure on the ground, clad in white flannel, a white helmet on his head, bearing a white umbrella with green lining, and retailing his generally improving reflections to an admiring audience . . .' as a contemporary put it) Lawford schemed and saw to fruition a ladies' championship event, to be held in harness with the men's championships.

The first of the ladies' singles was held in 1884. It was a leisurely affair, the more so as the distinguished charmers participating were weighed down by heavy dresses over multi-petticoats, and were permitted to simper or take a rest if their service broke down. The first ladies' title was taken by a Miss Maud Watson, who defeated a Miss L. Watson (*'snap!'* said the wags) in a final that provided more titters than jitters. Although Miss Maud of the Watson clan was to repeat her success in the following year, dedicated young females (who did not mind casting a clout or two in the interests of success) were also coming to the fore. Among them, the girl she vanquished, Miss Bingley, was to become a future lady champion six times over, as Mrs G. W. Hillyard.

Even more astonishing, the fourth ladies' singles title, in 1887, was convincingly won, at the record age of 15 years, by a Miss Lottie Dod – the first young female player in the world to learn to volley and smash effectively. A most accomplished all-round athlete, who was many, many years ahead of her time, Miss Dod went on to win Wimbledon five times before retiring from tennis in her twenties to take up golf full-time and to become English champion.

Lawford came up with another winning Wimbledon idea during the 'eighties, but was turned down time and time again by his normally-responsive co-members of the committee. This was for a Veterans' Championship. It was strange that no one could see it as a crowd-puller, because, from the time it was introduced into the annual tournament much later, it became one of the great attractions of Wimbledon, as indeed it is today.

Anyway, the odd and oddly-arrogant Henry Jones (who was wont to have it noted in the club's minutes that: 'the committee, having selected the best seats in the grandstand for themselves and their friends, adjourned to watch play . . .') was too busy pursuing a revolutionary idea of his own to have time to discuss Veterans with Lawford. Jones's un-Victorian notion was to open the club seven days a week, in order that lawn tennis could be played on Sundays. Somehow he persuaded enough members of the committee to back him for this unheard-of innovation, and, despite the protests of wealthy residents nearby, he got his way for some years from 1889. That he was a forceful, as well as an eccentric, personality is underlined in the minute of the club which quotes him as saying that it had been decided to decline to sacrifice 'the convenience of the members to the Sabbatarian prejudices of adjoining occupiers.'

Paradoxically, in the mid-'eighties, as the attendance figures shot up, the number of entrants for the championships went down. In 1885, when no fewer than 3,500 spectators watched the challenge rounds of the singles, there were only 23 challengers taking part. It would seem that the main reason for this was that the Renshaw twins were by now achieving such standards of 'professionalism' as amateurs that they were frightening away all but the keenest of opponents. They were certainly working constantly to improve their game, to the point that, at the end of the English lawn tennis season, they would sally forth together to the south of France, where they could practise throughout the winter. As gentlemen of leisure, they could afford to top up their skills in this way and so impress less-favoured natives at home and abroad.

The twins were also accomplished doubles players, and were winning so often that the rules of Wimbledon were changed for them in 1886 so that the men's doubles (as was to be the case, too, with the ladies' singles) were given challenge rounds – meaning that the holders (the Renshaws) did not have to play their way through the event. In fact, the brothers set another record in that decade when they won the Wimbledon doubles seven times between the event's inception in 1880 and the year when they began to fade, 1889. It is appealing to note that one of their three doubles defeats in those years was achieved by the Hon. Patrick Bowes-Lyon, a close relative of the family of Queen Elizabeth the Queen-Mother; he was partnered by Mr H. W. W. Wilberforce (subsequently Sir Herbert Wilberforce), who was to become club secretary in succession to Julian Marshall. The blood was still mainly 'blue' in and around the All-England Club and would remain so for many years to come.

The two Renshaws had also made history as participants in the first-ever international lawn tennis match, held at Wimbledon in 1883, when they convincingly defeated the Clark brothers of America before a distinguished crowd.

Generally speaking, the calculated preparation of the Newcombe-like mustachioed Renshaws, whose followers included female fans of almost devouringly-ferocious enthusiasms, did as much for tennis-playing in its early days as Wimbledon did for its administration and showmanship. Both twins were powerfully-built young men whose stamina was greater than that of most opponents they encountered. They were also accomplished strategists and good stroke players. Willie possessed one of the earliest power-play services of the game and could also take the ball early with his ground strokes instead of on the drop. He was first rate at the net and was sound overhead. Ernest was a more delicate and sensitive player, possessing most of the strokes and using them with a smoother and more graceful style. Both were capable, when the occasion demanded, of developing all-court volleying attacks.

Through their intelligent use of the full court and of the lower net (from 1882), the Renshaws undoubtedly steered English tennis towards its early successful natural game, based on ground-stroke play – adding up to the first identifiable lawn tennis style in the world.

The Wimbledon committee (now strengthened by a full-time treasurer, a Mr Arthur Chitty) was also forging ahead in various ways and made another important innovation when it introduced a tarpaulin to the Centre Court in the 1885 championships. This vital piece of anti-weather equipment, which would never again be absent from the Wimbledon fortnight, was initially hired at £8 per season, but in the following year it was deemed prudent to purchase two sheets for use on the two principal courts.

The turf at Worple Road had been much admired over the years, but there had been feelings among the perfectionists of the committee that it could be even better, so 'the best local gardener that money could buy' was sought in 1887, and he was found in the cultivated person of Thomas Coleman, who was to play a vital part, for 40 years thereafter, in maintaining the emerald turves of the Wimbledon lawn tennis courts in a state of perfection unchallenged and unrivalled anywhere in the world. Mr Coleman invariably stabled a horse on the ground and used it to do all mowing and rolling, using specialised harness for each purpose. His various horses over the years were trained to wear special strapped-on boots, like elephants feet, to avoid cutting or damaging the precious turves in any way. The poor gardener and his animal had to put up with much ribald mockery ('sold his tusks, old man?') from members, as well as from small boys of the area who knew there was always some fun to be had in the holidays at the four-acre 'circus' in Worple Road.

These excitements and excursions were symptomatic of a lawn tennis fever that was spreading from London and the south-east to most parts of the British Isles. Inevitably, it had its resentments and reactions. So popular had the annual Wimbledon fortnight become by 1887 that sundry jealousies were finding expressions in various ways, such as letters to the editors of regional newspapers suggesting that the so-called All-England committee had become too powerful for its tennis boots, and that the time had come for a court revolution. In particular, the grumblers opined, a national governing body, as had long existed in America, should be set up 'to clip certain wings at Wimbledon' and to take overall responsibility for and control of the blossoming game.

There had been envious rumblings of this sort before, and Mr Jones was too busy publicising Miss Lottie Dod's fantastic succcess in the still-new women's singles to be bothered with the new campaign that got going during the 1887 season. But he had to take notice later the same year when two nationally-respected figures in the game outside Wimbledon took it upon themselves to sound out tennis opinion throughout the British Isles. They were Mr H. S. Scrivener, president of Oxford University Lawn Tennis Club, and Mr G. W. Hillyard, of the Marylebone Cricket Club (a man destined to be a future secretary at Wimbledon, and whose wife was to become one of the great women players of the era). After much deliberation, these two self-important young bloods concocted a letter weighted against Wimbledon, which they circulated in the pre-Christmas mail of 1887, inviting all interested parties to attend a meeting at the Freemasons' Tavern, London, on 26 January, 1888.

The get-together proved to be stormy, but timely and fruitful. The pub was loud with voices from Scotland and Wales as well as from all parts of England. The Wimbledon 'characters' were present in force, fairly sure that whatever developed they would still be able to exert a main influence. There were the usual rambling speeches, and chips were exhibited on sundry muscular shoulders. Grievances against the All-England Club's 'autocratic mismanagement of the game' were aired by the hour. But in the end, although most criticisms had been answered and a lot of common sense talked by representatives of the Wimbledon pioneers, it was very obvious that virtually everyone from outside London wanted to see a new all-British body founded, in addition to the All-England Club. When, in the concluding stages of the meeting, Captain Hobbs, of the Northern Lawn Tennis Association (just one of a host of Army officers present, who still seemed to be dominating the administration of the game) proposed that an association be formed 'in the best interests of the game', made up of the delegates of all clubs and associations present at the meeting, the resolution was carried to loud applause, and all the leading clubs indicated their willingness to support such a body. As much on the principal that 'if you can't beat 'em, join 'em,' as anything else, the warriors of Wimbledon went along with the new move. And their reward came, in April, 1888, when it was announced that William Renshaw (whose name at that time was synonymous with Wimbledon) was to be first president of the new British Lawn Tennis Association.

Mr H. Chipp, of the Chiswick Park Lawn Tennis Club, was elected first honorary secretary, and his scrupulously clear minutes are still available at L.T.A. headquarters.

Willie Renshaw whose name (with that of his brother) has since 1904 been remembered in a trophy presented each year to the Wimbledon singles' champion, was destined to die young (predeceased by his twin, Ernest). But he reigned for a few years as an excellent first president of the new national association, and begat a distinguished band of high-born but far-seeing successors, in the Earl of Cavan, Mr W. H. Collins, Lord Desborough, Viscount d'Abernon, Sir Samuel Hoare, Viscount Templewood, the Duke of Devonshire and Sir Carl Aarvold.

Fortuitously, the setting-up of the L.T.A. came at the right time for the All-England Club, which was able to shed the more irksome of its worrysome tasks and concentrate on the main 'plus', the presenting and nourishing of the greatest tournament of its kind in the tennis world. Under Renshaw's direction, the governing body soon made it clear that it was no threat to Wimbledon as 'club of clubs'. The L.T.A. would not seek to dictate policy, but rather to advise, help and guide all who were playing the game. Indeed, the main objective of the association was stated to be 'to advance and safeguard the interests of lawn tennis'.

In seeking to establish overall control of the game, it was essential that the L.T.A. should remove from the keeping of the All-England Lawn Tennis Club (unassailably still the premier club in the world) the rules it had created, after in turn inheriting them from Major Wingfield, through the Marylebone Cricket Club. This delicate matter was achieved, thanks largely to Willie Renshaw's good offices and sound common sense. All claims to hold or own copyright in lawn tennis's rule book were relinquished by the Wimbledon pioneers within weeks of the new association being established, so that the way was clear for the L.T.A. to publish its first Rules of Lawn Tennis in 1889, thereby also to set its stamp on the game in many overseas countries as well as in the British Isles.

As has been mentioned earlier, the three wise men of the

All-England Club had done a superb job in drafting their version of the rules of the game and there was little that the L.T.A. could add or subtract. Inevitably, foreign associations wanted to have their say in getting the widely-recognised 'English' rules altered to suit their local books, and as a means of showing their own power. In particular, the United States L.T.A. lobbied powerfully at once for the idea that players should change ends after alternate games. This was rejected out of hand, but it is fascinating to find that less than a year later, the 'English' L.T.A. had agreed that the players should change ends after every set, subject to an appeal to the umpire.

In Britain, too, people were always ready to put forward evidence that changes were desirable. As a result of representations, many alterations in the rules of the game were contemplated, but no more were in fact to be made until 1898, when the service rule was amended to allow the server 'to walk up to the baseline immediately preceding the delivery of his service'. Wimbledon had done its job so well that not even the interfering nigglers who used the sharpest of fine-toothed combs to go through the rule book could find true fault.

Although it is worth noting in passing that it would have nothing to do with the ladies' game until 1899, one good thing the new L.T.A. initiated was an increasing number of inter-club and inter-county matches and other competitions. Indeed, within ten years it had sanctioned over 70 tournaments, which compares very favourably with the 80 or so played today. But with all this fresh activity, it was still towards Wimbledon that most players' eyes turned, as Mohammed's faithful turn to Mecca.

At the height of the lawn tennis season in the year that the L.T.A. was establishing itself, its distinguished president was taking part in one of the most remarkable matches ever played on the Centre Court of the All-England Club. This was the final of the 1889 All-Comers' singles (the winner of which was to play the defending singles' champion, who that year was twin Ernest, as it happened). Willie Renshaw's opponent was H. S. Barlow, a fine stroke player who was coming into his prime at the same rate as the great champion, William, was waning.

If Barlow had a fault, it was in finishing; he tended to lack the ginger required to win matches. Nevertheless, he started brilliantly on this occasion, won the first two sets from Renshaw at 6–3, 7–5, and led for most of the vital third, only to see it saved by William at 8–6. In the fourth set, Barlow again steadily advanced until he held a commanding 5–2 lead. He held match point no fewer than six times, only for William to save the day each time. The sixth 'save' was perhaps the most remarkable and characteristic. At match point Willie fumbled and dropped his racket during the rally, as he was positioned at the net. Barlow, the sensitive stroke player, instead of playing a simple drive, which would have given him the match, chose to deliver the coup de grace with style by lobbing the ball neatly over 'the master's' head. It was a fatal mistake against so gifted a player. Acrobatically, Willie scooped up his racket while hurtling backwards, retrieved the lob as it dropped to the baseline and passed Barlow with it, before winning the set, 10–8.

But there was greater drama to come. In the fifth set, Barlow again went ahead and seemed in an unbeatable position when he took the first five games to nil. At this point, a gentleman in the stand offered to wager 100 sovereigns to one against Willie winning the match, but could find no takers.

Amazingly, although Barlow was to hold three more match points in the course of the final set, Willie Renshaw held on and doggedly drew himself up to five-all before striding on to win through at 8–6 as a prelude to beating brother Ernest in the challenge round next day and capturing his seventh singles' title the hard way.

Fortunes at the All-England Club, alas, failed to maintain an upward climb in the 1890s. The retirement of the Renshaw twins had coincided with a bicycling craze and with an invasion by talented Irish tennis players, who failed to draw the crowds in the way that native English stars had done. Wimbledon temporarily lost some of its magic in the early 'nineties, and failed to recover fully until another great English family pair, the astonishing Doherty brothers, came on the scene towards the turn of the century. In the interim, Henry Jones and his merry, haughty men had had to keep very much quieter than heretofore. Indeed, croquet was even re-introduced in 1896 to help subscription income.

The reign of the Dohertys (which began in 1897, when R. F. Doherty won the singles' title, and was to last for nearly ten years) not only revived the fortunes of the All-England Club but also acted as a further stimulant to the spread of lawn tennis in England and throughout the world. Indeed, before the long reign of Queen Victoria had ended in 1901, Wimbledon was witnessing crowd scenes such as few sports had ever enjoyed (so much so that, in 1901 Slazengers began their long and continuing run of support for Wimbledon in supplying championship balls – foretelling sponsorships that were bound to come) while in the most remote parts of her Empire (and particularly in the new Dominion of Australia) news of the Doherty successes was inspiring young men to practice assiduously, in the hope of being able to play at Wimbledon, as well as to get local tournaments going at which to show off their prowess and perhaps find patrons.

The handsome Doherty brothers, their wavy black hair parted in the centre, were in their early twenties when they first took Wimbledon by storm. R. F. (Reggie) Doherty was born in 1874, and his brother, H. L. (Laurie) Doherty in 1876. They had so much talent that between them they carried off nearly every prize in singles and doubles between 1897 and 1906 (as well as securing the Davis Cup for Britain on four consecutive occasions, from 1903 to 1906 ... and as well as Laurie's achievement in winning the U.S. singles in 1903 – the first foreigner to do so. The young Dohertys had learned to play in the English manner, as perfected by the Renshaws, and had refused to be influenced by the special grips for forehand and backhand being lauded in America, and in Europe, where French and German championship tournaments had begun to be played in the 'nineties. They had first been inspired to play by their elder brother, the Rev. W. V. Doherty, when still at Cambridge. They were rich enough to follow the Renshaw tradition of wintering on the Riviera and were privileged to make full use of the court at Cannes that the Renshaws had built for themselves.

Reggie won the Wimbledon singles four times in succession, beating H. S. Mahoney, his brother Laurie, A. W. Gore and S. H. Smith in the challenge rounds. Laurie, in turn won it five times, defeating A. W. Gore, F. L. Riseley (thrice) and N. E. Brookes.

The Press came alive to the nuances of style that lawn tennis was by now achieving when its readers began demanding more and more inches of coverage on the Doherty techniques. Some players, by their magic, make every rabbit feel he could be a fox. That was the effect R. F. and H. L. had on week-end players, from Penge to Plymouth. Schoolboys and office boys were also affected, which is a sure sign of 'the common touch' in sport. More grandmothers 'died' in June in the late 1890s and early 1900s than in the foggiest of winters.

Both Dohertys were superbly elegant stroke players. Would-be champions could get the latest in rackets from Harrods, dazzlingly white shoes from Lillywhites and immaculate flannels from Savile Row. But where could they buy a selection of groundstrokes? Nowhere, save by queuing to see the new masters in play on the Centre Court of the All-England Club.

There was little to choose between Laurie Doherty and his elder brother, Reggie, although some say Laurie was the greatest match player of all time – even greater than Tilden in the same sort of way. Reggie was an even more complete stroke player than his brother but was less a 'killer' because of ill-health. Alas, like the Renshaws before them, both Doherty brothers died young, of ill-health, during World War I.

The *wrong* day to go and see them was when they played against each other. Like the Renshaws, they hated having to decide such a tussle; both tended to play below par, not wishing to rob the other; and most of their brother-against-brother matches were reported to be 'colourless' and 'uninspiring'. But in playing doubles together, they invariably rose to the occasion, following their services to the net and volleying from below net height. In receiving, in turn, their policy was a new one then (but an accepted one today) of the receiver attacking aggressively instead of leaning on a safe return.

The Americans were visiting Wimbledon more and more during the great years of the Dohertys. Most of their best players in this period were essentially volleyers, but the secret weapon they sought to use to ace the English stars was the top-spin service, which astonished players who had not experienced it by swerving and breaking back at great speed. Laurie Doherty was the first to find that there was an answer to the U.S. weapon. He felt out the spinning ball by playing every service (including every service fault) back into court, and in no time he found that he could stand in and take the top-spin ball on the rise. Such was the wonder of Laurie's singles' play that, by 1904, the crowds at the championships were so dense that profits in excess of £1,400 were being made.

In all, the Dohertys won nine Wimbledon singles between them and eight doubles. They were the greatest of all the early English stars and did much to push the game into the twentieth century. They were studied as much by overseas players as by the home breed, and after their retirement in 1906, all three Wimbledon championships were won by overseas players. But it did not greatly matter any more as far as the international acceptance of Wimbledon was concerned. The Dohertys had finally made Wimbledon, financially and prestigiously. It would never look back.

Chapter Two / Thirty years ... and Thirty

Although she is known to have wielded a racket on the lawns of Balmoral, Queen Victoria never gave any public display of interest in tennis, and never went to Wimbledon. Royalty began to take its carefully carved out place in the courtside royal box at Worple Road from 1907. The timing was right in one respect, for the fine lawns, which so commanded display, were surrounded by fawning crowds, eager for excitement and spectacle during the championship fortnight and on other special occasions. It was wrong in another respect in that, after thirty years of English dominance of lawn tennis, almost from the moment the first royals arrived the native challenge began to go into a decline from which it would not recover for another thirty years (during which time there would be but five British singles winners).

All three championships in 1907, in fact, went to 'foreigners' (if Empire stalwarts could be included in such a category); the men's singles was convincingly won by Brookes of Australia; the ladies' singles went to America's Miss May Sutton (later to play on as Mrs Bundy); and the doubles was taken by Brookes, paired with Wilding of New Zealand. The unruffled sun of those halcyon days was continuing not to set on the great British Empire, so it was considered right, proper and noble that the Brookes/Wilding efforts should be given the bounteous blessing of royal visits by the Prince of Wales and his Princess. Indeed, the heir to the throne was so impressed by the quality of the game and its administration at Wimbledon that he thereupon accepted the presidency of the All-England Club, and also presented a magnificent challenge cup to be awarded annually to the winner of the men's singles.

The Americans (supported by hundreds of tennis-mad tourists) were beginning to make their presence felt, with star material in red-haired M. A. McLoughlin, Beals Wright and others; some Continentals were beginning to make their marks, too, notably German's strong Otto Froitzheim and France's temperamental but brilliant A. H. Gobert.

The foreign invasion of Wimbledon was strong numerically as well as in its skills, as players from many countries sought to bloody the lion's nose in its own den, or to show off their 'professional' techniques at the greatest tournament of all and before the most knowledgeable crowd to be found anywhere. Indeed, the draws for the men's singles were steadily increasing, to the point that by 1910 there would be no fewer than 92 participants, while in 1911 the record would be broken once more, with a field of 104 from 17 nations taking part in the same event.

Attendances, too, were steadily on the up and up. The public loved the new names and the new excitements, as this celebrity or that character was tipped as the next champion. In effect, however, from 1907 until the beginning of the First World War, the foreign contenders were mainly kept at bay by the superiority of the two Australasians, A. F. Wilding and N. E. Brookes, and by a solitary, stubborn Englishman, A. W. Gore (no relation to Wimbledon's pioneer of the same name). Indeed, despite challenge after challenge in the final rounds, the singles championship never went outside the British Empire in those years, although the doubles were snatched once by the French champions, A. H. Gobert and Max Decugis, in 1911.

Among the controversies of the day was the question whether or not the holder of the championship should be required to play through, or whether he should be exempt from the all-comers' competition (as had long been the rule) and merely have to play the winner of the competition in the all-important challenge round. Equally, there were points in favour and points against, and the arguments were endless.

The Lawn Tennis Association was far from happy about the long-standing All-England arrangement and wanted a revision so that playing through could be established as a feature of the Wimbledon fortnight, on the principle that this would make for surprises and for a fairer final. A circular query to 142 of the leading players produced the interesting response that 68 were in favour of playing through, while 46 wanted to retain the challenge round; and (in addition to two who failed to sign their papers) there were 26 'don't knows'. As a consequence of the questionnaire, the committee dithered. No decision was made in the matter, and, alas, the old method was continued until a few years after the First World War, by which time the championships had moved to another part of Wimbledon.

There was also a tremendous stir of controversy, in the last years of Worple Road, when accusations were made at the A.G.M. of the L.T.A. by a member of the All-England Club, who accused certain members of the Wimbledon All-England committee of accepting bribes to have a new ball manufacturer admitted to the championships. But, after the matter had dragged on for many months, when an enquiry was set up before Mr Justice Shearman the accuser failed to appear, and the committee men were exonerated. Under an agreement, signed in 1908 with leading manufacturers, by arrangement with the L.T.A., balls were supplied for tournament use at six shillings per dozen (as against the retail price of twelve shillings) and the manufacturers refunded a royalty of 9d. per dozen balls. This arrangement was continued.

Spot tests on balls had already been introduced, and these were strengthened in due course by more rigorous inspections of the manufactured product, to ensure uniform weight and bounce at all tournaments.

Norman Brookes, who had so many tricks up his immaculate sleeves that he was known as the Wizard, was the first of the lawn tennis giants to step into the Victorian-turned-Edwardian shoes of the Doherty brothers and to be taken to the hearts of the Wimbledon crowds. A first-rate all-rounder (who could have excelled equally in cricket or golf, on both of which he was keen) Brookes was to be rated by Tilden the greatest match player in the first fifty years of lawn tennis. An Australian, born in the first year of Wimbledon, 1877, he had made history early by being the first overseas player to appear in the challenge round at Worple Road. That had been in 1905. In 1907 he formally took over the crown from the Dohertys.

Volleying was Brookes' forte, and anticipation reinforced his talent. In the main, the style he followed was the 'new' American one, and his service was entirely derived from U.S. experience and observation. An aggressive but controlled hitter of the ball, he was a tactician and strategian rather than a brilliant stroke player. If he had a fault, it was that he tended to fade in very long matches because of some inherent lack of stamina, but to counter this he developed the endearing habit of drinking vintage champagne between sets (as if it were barley water) to keep up his strength. That there was nothing basically wrong with Brookes' constitution, however, was to be underlined in due course. Gonzales-like, he would soldier on brilliantly, until he was well into his forties, and would extend players of Tilden's talent, even then, by the almost uncanny anticipation and deadly volleying he would still command.

It has been said, and it may be true, that Brookes' greatest advantage was that he was left-handed in an age when this was rare among tennis players (and certainly there would not be another sinistral player of top talent until Drobney in the 'fifties). But by any measure of talent and stature, Norman Brookes (later to be knighted) was a giant of his time.

On his way to his 1907 success, Brookes had appropriately been taken to five sets by his seven-year-younger competitor from New Zealand, Tony Wilding, who would in due course scale almost equal heights of acclaim, but from a totally different stance. The Kiwi was half-a-head taller than the Aussie and adopted a base-line power game, stemming from his own skills, whereas Brookes would advance to the net at the slightest excuse, thence to 'read' and capitalise on his opponents' weaknesses.

In the first of Wilding's singles wins at Wimbledon, in 1910, he beat A. W. Gore, the sole outstanding Englishman of the time. This was the Arthur Gore who had won the singles as long ago as 1901 (against R. F. Doherty) and again in 1908 and 1909. Of Laver build, but with a thick black moustache, Gore was a fighter of the first order, with a tremendously strong forehand, but there seems little doubt that his later successes would have been less likely had not Norman Brookes decided to remain in Australia during the appropriate years.

Astonishingly, Arthur Gore, who could fight like a dervish when his limited armoury of shots set his back to the wall, was a veteran of 41 when he won his last Wimbledon singles title in 1909, and would go on to compete uniquely in a total of 29 consecutive tournaments by the time of his retirement. He would also achieve in due course the signal honour (at the age of 58) of defeating the Duke of York in Wimbledon's 50th Jubilee championships in 1926 – which was certainly a story to drink out on for years!

Wilding followed Gore as champion in the four consecutive years after 1909 ... whereupon Brookes chose to arrive from Australia, to teach the younger man who exactly was master by defeating him in a great final in 1914. He did it partly by good and varied serving, but chiefly by aggressive volleying, in which he had always followed the advice of his 'discoverer', Dr Eaves, who was given to saying: 'Rush the top of the net and stay there'.

Wilding, although considered a thorough sportsman in every way, had tended to disparage Brookes, when asked for an opinion, in the period when they were not in direct conflict (although they were highly successful doubles players together for several years in the Davis Cup) – this to the point of saying that the Australian was over-rated in the memories of his English supporters, and that Brookes chose to stay 'down under' because the real opposition was now in Europe. That this was nonsense as far as grass was concerned, at any rate, was quickly proved when the two men met in the challenge round in 1914, after Brookes had knocked out the German champion, Otto Froitzheim, at the all-comers' stage.

The difference between them was certainly not as great, as Brookes' straight sets' victory (as against the five set margin when they had last met at Wimbledon) might seem to imply. But it was a statesmanslike and salutory thrashing that he administered, nonetheless.

Wilding, who was the type of player who needed hard work to bring out his best game, protested that he was below his best on the day, because he had asked to be allowed to play through the competition as a means of warming up to the final, but this had been refused by the committee on the grounds that he was the holder.

When the two giants (both over six feet, with Wilding the taller by several inches) finally faced each other on the fabled centre court, Wilding started so hesitantly that Brookes broke service twice to lead 4–0, and, although the younger man fought back to save the set and reached 3–4 and 40–15, he soon began

B

to slip again. Brookes' service was consistently powerful and accurate, and featured four different styles of delivery; his volleying was subtle and deadly; and, in the second and third sets, Wilding inexplicably tried lobbing to the forehand of his left-handed opponent, with fatal results, because Brookes was strongest when he volleyed and smashed from the forehand.

So in the end the Australian (having slaughtered the German) defeated the New Zealander convincingly in front of a mainly-English crowd, as part of one of the last international sporting occasions that would be held for four long, bitter years.

Contrarily, and pleasantly so, the ladies' singles over the period were still dominated by native Englishwomen, with the solitary exception of America's Miss May Sutton's surprise win in 1907. Mrs Lambert Chambers (a previous multiple winner, as Miss D. K. Douglas) was queen of the courts until the First World War, taking the title four times, to give her an all-time total of seven wins – an achievement unparalleled until 1938, when the incomparable Mrs Helen Wills-Moody at last surpassed it.

Mrs Chambers was indeed, in her day, the finest woman player in the world (followed by Miss Sutton of the U.S., the Mistresses Larcombe, Hillyard and Sterry of England, and Miss Martin of Ireland). But credit for this English domination was given all-too-grudgingly by the men of the day – spectators as well as players. It was fashionable to decry the efforts of the women around lawn tennis clubs in general and at Wimbledon in particular. English lady players of the period were admired abroad as the greatest in the game. But they could have been even further ahead of the opposition had they been allowed (as were most of their American and Continental opponents) to play and practice with top Englishmen. Incredibly, such a thing was mainly frowned on at Wimbledon until the 'twenties, so it is little wonder that the suffragette movement claimed so many supporters among sportswomen.

This was indeed the period when pioneer suffragettes were on the march and men were reacting in stuffy fashion, to say the least. One of the main publicity points in the programme of the female emancipators was for guerrillas to strike at clubhouses or any buildings that could be considered to be male preserves.

New permanent wooden stands had been built around Wimbledon's Centre Court, at a cost of £1,200, and these were very much the pride and joy of the All-England Committee. They were also potentially ideal material for fire-raising. So, when someone pointed out that the stands seemed to offer convenient tinder for the violently-inclined women, the club secretary, Mr George Hillyard (whose wife, a prominent tennis player, was *'not* a member of the suffragettes', he assured the committee) hit the roof. But he was well advised enough to hire a beefy ex-R.A. sergeant to act as night watchman.

This timely tip-off (believed to have originated with a member whose wife was involved in the plot) and its defensive reflex took place just in time. On the second night that the watchman was on duty, the suffragettes struck at Wimbledon. Somehow they had succeeded earlier in smuggling inflammable substances into the ground and had planted them under the main stand. They were on the very point of striking the match that would have sent that year's championship up in smoke when the watchman crept up on them. The subsequent chase was worthy of the Keystone Cops, and at the end of it a female prisoner was taken to and remanded at Wimbledon Police Station 'for further enquiries'. In a public ceremony the next day, the alert watchman was presented with a golden sovereign, at which he announced that, if that was the going rate for suffragettes, he could be depended upon to round up more as the opportunities presented themselves. But they never did and he never did. Wimbledon was evidently struck off the list of targets.

Meanwhile, as a small gesture to progress, ladies' doubles and mixed doubles were introduced into the championship fortnight in 1913 for the first time, but there was little interest in them in terms of spectator response before the war. One reason for this was undoubtedly the fact that virtually no women knew how to volley in those days (although there were whispers that a new star-in-the-making, a 15-year-old, Mlle. Suzanne Lenglen, was skittling over experienced players around the south of France and using volleying techniques worthy of a man.

The introduction of the two new Wimbledon events had come about primarily because in 1913 the International Lawn Tennis Federation (which had been founded the previous year in Paris, with the English association playing a leading part) had granted the titles of World Grasscourt Championships to Wimbledon (while conferring the World Hardcourt titles on Paris). Unlike

Wimbledon, Paris had chosen to restrict the French singles' titles to French nationals (while adding the World Singles' titles as open events). The native restriction was to be rescinded in 1925, and the world championships themselves would cease, as such, in 1923. But whatever the changes, introduced by national and international bodies, Wimbledon would never be in any danger of being accepted by players and public alike as other than the greatest lawn tennis centre in the world.

In 1913, all previous attendance records were smashed at Wimbledon (with touts selling £1 tickets on men's finals day at £10 a time and queues half-a-mile long coiling round Worple Road and beyond). The beloved stands, which had at one time looked more than adequate for the greatest attraction the game could put on, now appeared woefully small, with their 2,000 capacity and their top 'take' of about £2,000.

Appropriately, finals day was American Independence Day, 4 July, because the big attraction was the 'Californian Comet', Maurice McLoughlin versus the 'Kiwi Killer', Anthony Wilding.

Wilding, who played in an individual but mainly Eastern style, had been 'king' of Wimbledon in the absence of Norman Brookes, and was favourite to win for the fourth time running. Maurice McLoughlin, his ferocious opponent, was nonetheless highly regarded as the world's greatest exponent of the Western American style of powered stroke-making, as had been developed on the west coast of America where concrete courts were most common, but it was not thought that the U.S. champion could beard the 'Britisher' in his den and win.

McLoughlin in fact surprised everyone by rocketing to 5–3 in the first set, with his service (his strongest suit) to follow for the match. But Wilding, who had been nonplussed at first by the heavy topspin style of the tall American and by his flat, devastating service, was beginning to settle and was even finding answers at this stage. After a very long game, Wilding broke McLoughlin's service to hold on at 4–5 . . . and somehow went on to take the set 8–6. This gave the Kiwi the boost his confidence needed. He won the second set 6–3, having led 4–1 at one point. But McLoughlin rallied impressively in the third set. By constantly storming the net, he turned Wilding's 4–2 lead into one of 5–4 in his own favour. The following games went with the service until McLoughlin was 8–7 in the lead. Wilding then took a game against service and, ahead by 9–8, was at match point when he was foot-faulted. A lesser player might have let such a climacteric upset throw him, but not so the Wimbledon singles holder. Tony Wilding, one of the fittest men in sport, quickly recovered his composure and forced the next two points for the match, 8–6, 6–3, 10–8.

The Wilding win (his fourth in a row) was a most popular one. The New Zealander was a physical fitness fanatic, in the Sedgman mould, who presented the glowing-with-health appearance men and women found most appealing in their athletic heroes. Alas, he was to die in a trench at Neuve Chapelle a few months after the outbreak of war, before he had really reached his peak as a tennis player. When he had first played at Wimbledon, in 1904, Wilding (whose father had been born in the West Country and had set an English public schools record in the long jump) had just arrived at Cambridge and had been undecided whether to concentrate on tennis or cricket, at which he was equally good.

The war began, in fact, at the wrong moment for lawn tennis and for Wimbledon. A matter of weeks before hostilities got under way, the All-England Committee (under its new-found royal patronge) had decided that the Wimbledon championships had outgrown the Worple Road ground and it had been casting around for a suitable new site at the very moment when the Kaiser decreed that there would be no more amateur sport until 1918 or later.

But any misgivings the committee might have had that the five-year lapse would cause the public to lose interest would soon be dispelled, as the 'teen years were superseded by the 'twenties. In its first 40 years, lawn tennis had made fantastic progress, to the point that it had become perhaps *the* most international of all games. And for this it had Wimbledon to thank more than any other place or factor. But, in the 50 years from the end of the first war, the progress would be even more astounding and the cornerstone position of the new Wimbledon would be even more assured.

Chapter Three / Lenglen trail a-winding

Lawn tennis has always had its brilliant 'loners', perhaps to a greater degree than any other sport. One such was Bill Tilden, the new lawn tennis name to be reckoned with immediately after the war. He was also the very first American to win Wimbledon, and he did it in 1920. This was the year the site for the proposed new All-England Club was found, but not occupied, in Church Road, to the other side of the railway station and just two miles from the original ground in Worple Road. The move would have taken place many years before, had it not been for the war. It had been clear by 1913 that a commodious new prestige location would have to be found, featuring several times as much space for spectators, if the club was to retain its international and national leadership in the game.

Instead, in the circumstances of war, the Worple Road premises had assumed an unreal, twilight air between 1914 and 1918. After the 1914 fortnight, the championships had been suspended; members of military age had gone off on active service and had been given free membership when on leave; enemy nationals had been ceremoniously drummed out of the club; and staff had been cut to a minimum as part of a very necessary economy drive; even the motor-mower, which had taken over from the horses a few years before, went to war. And although wealthy patrons had chipped in donations totalling about £15,000, the entire place had taken on a rather seedy, run-down aspect by the time members were drifting back from the Services in the spring of 1919.

The sole way in which things had improved rather than deteriorated was that public interest in law tennis was greater than ever. Weary of war but eager for the drama of the sporting fray at international levels denied the world for years, people clamoured for seats for the 1919 championship meeting on a scale that made 1913's scenes seem like a nursery school revolt.

There was also such an unprecedentedly large entry of players that it became necessary for the first time to set up an elimination committee, with controversial powers to 'hire and fire' applicants. This caused much criticism in the Press and unhappiness among the players. Indeed, it soon became obvious that only a system of eliminations based on pre-tournament competition would be just, but there was too much else going on for any such thing to be introduced at that time and, temporarily at least, injustices had to be endured.

Before Tilden established himself as a star-of-stars at Wimbledon, there was Lenglen. She was a woman, and up to that time it had been the 'characters' among the men who had traditionally drawn the largest crowds to Wimbledon. Suzanne Lenglen was to change all that. The first and only Frenchwoman to win the Championship at Wimbledon, she had the sort of magic that commands a following and the 'common touch' that holds it once it has been commanded.

The year 1919, when Lenglen scored her first great Wimbledon victory, was not an outstanding year in the men's singles, as virtually no one of the top stars who had survived the war was yet seriously in training. Despite this, so glad were they to have even a pale shadow of the great days of pre-war tennis, the spectators chose not to be too critical, and cheered every ace as if it were the greatest achievement in the world. Brookes (the holder) went out to fellow-Australian G. L. (Gerald) Patterson, 6–3, 7–5, 6–2, in three sets of not very inspiring tennis.

In contrast, the challenge round final of the women's singles turned out to be one of the matches of the century, with both women fighting fit and determined to win. Indeed, it possessed all the drama and passions that made for a tremendous three-act play, with an old queen versus a new queen, and a sharply-divided populace.

This apart, the ladies' singles match had many things going for it from the start.

It was the veteran against the prodigy, the mature Mrs Lambert

Chambers (née Douglass) being the holder. Mrs L. C. had won the championship seven times, and was rated the greatest-woman-player-ever on grass. By contrast, Suzanne Lenglen was barely 20 and had never played on grass before in her life. Born at Compeigney in Picardy in May, 1899, she was visiting England at the behest of her father, Charles Lenglen, who was also her trainer and who coached her from the sidelines during matches in a way that would never be allowed today.

It was England versus France, at a time when national pride needed a boost, despite the victory the allies had won over Germany. The war had been stunning in its bloody slaughter for France and England, rather than a triumph. Sport was different – clean-cut and decisive. Also, France had been cheekily claiming paternity of tennis (when every Englishman knew it was an English child) on the basis that 'tennis' stemmed from the word 'tenir' (meaning 'hold' or 'play') and on the grounds that she had been the home of tennis, when no one else wanted to know, from the Middle Ages, until upstart Wimbledon had changed the rules in the late nineteenth century.

It was before the greatest 'fans' in the land. The royal box contained King George V, Queen Mary, Princess Mary and a host of other near-gods (as they were then regarded). In response to this enlightened leadership, the stands were packed as never before, and the terraces resembled today's rush-hour crush on City platforms of London's underground railway. The cheers that greeted the arrival of 'the royals' were heard more than half-a-mile away and the whole town seemed to stir with the excitement of the occasion. Indeed, so great was the press of the populace around the royal party that the start of the final was held up for some time.

It was also something really new – women's suffrage in practical form: a young rebel showing a representative of the old school that a new era had dawned for women ... showing it in her clothes as well as her prowess. Mademoiselle from Picardy favoured scarves several yards long; multi-buttoned, long-sleeved, coloured cardigans; vividly-slashed lipsticks; and a series of turban-like coloured bandeaux, without which she was seldom seen, each kept in place by an expensively-glittering and regal diamond pin. Her English opponents (and especially Mrs Lambert Chambers) tended to favour eyeshields, weighty dresses and mannish blazers. Crowds then, as now, went to be seen as well as to see, and some of the women spectators inevitably copied the fashions worn by their star favourites. In this respect, it was a great relief and joy to younger fans to have a young fashion plate to follow, and French at that, in the Incomparable Suzanne, as she was to be named.

There is a legend (curiously nurtured here, as well as in France) that Mlle. Lenglen was beautiful as well as being immaculate and cute. A study of the many photographs of her that have survived certainly do not lend support to the idea. Graceful and charming, yes; beautiful, no. Contrary again to legend, she was quite a big girl. Not a carthorse, but not a sylph either. But most of all, she had a conk (to use colloquial parlance) that would have done credit to a suitable mate for Jimmy Durante. But, then, in her era, only the Spanish girl, Señorita Lili d'Alvarez, came anything near to being a beauty, on photographic evidence ... while even compared to the undistinguished others, Mrs Lambert Chambers was plain and formidable, with a huge, square face and massive shoulders. Legends may be legends, but some are false.

On the other hand, in the eyes of this beholder at least, there have never at any time been any truly beautiful girls among the first ranks of lawn tennis players (although what is my opinion worth when I record the fact that a good-looking, sophisticated young Englishman of my acquaintance recently confessed to having mad desires for Billie-Jean King?)

Suzanne did have good legs, however, and showed fairly lengthy parts of them, under pleated skirts, at a time when other players' tennis dresses were voluminous and lengthy. The news of her abilities and attractions had spread during the 1919 competition to the point that, as she progressed from round to round, the attendant crowds increased by leaps and bounds, their interest inflamed by nightly headlines in the London newspapers, saying: 'Long live Lenglen'; 'Suzanne does it again'; 'Wimbledon takes young French girl to its heart'; and, punnily, 'The Leglen trail'.

Her first opponent had been the experienced Mrs Cobb, who had had to pull out all the stops to win one game against the French girl; and in the second round, the great and famous Mrs Larcombe (a pre-war Wimbledon champion) had only been able to snatch three games from the net-playing Suzanne in the two quick sets. Nor did Suzanne's later opponents fare much better. In the third round, it was Mrs Cradock's turn to be reduced to the indignity of gaining only one game, while exactly the same cruel fate awaited the talented Mrs Godfree (then Miss McKane) in the quarter finals.

Mlle. Lenglen's opponent at the penultimate stage of the all-comers' competition had been Miss Elizabeth Ryan and, before the largest crowd yet, the young French girl had convincingly beaten the top American by 6–4 and 7–5. This had brought her, in turn, up against Miss Satterthwaite in an all-too-easy all-comers' final, which she romped through by 6–1, 6–1.

The challenge round final, against the reigning champion, had been arranged (as now) for the Friday of the second week of the Wimbledon fortnight, and a huge crowd had assembled by lunchtime, despite incessant rain, their massed umbrellas giving a seaside look to the courts. By mid-afternoon, after much telephoning to and from Buckingham Palace, it had been decided to postpone the match until the Saturday. It was a good decision. On the last day of the fortnight, the covers were removed in warm sunshine, to the accompaniment of a light drying wind. Conditions were perfect by the time the veteran (who had first won on the centre court 16 years before) and the prodigy (showing no signs of nerves) began to knock up on the close-cropped, baize-like, fast-playing surface of the Centre Court.

Mrs Lambert Chambers was wearing her usual tent-like garment, with multi-undergarments, so there was inevitably a gasp of shocked surprise when Mlle. Lenglen appeared in a simple, short-sleeved one-piece dress, the skirt of which, just below the knees, allowed considerable freedom of movement. Indeed, from the moment of Suzanne's appearance, the younger elements of the vast crowd stopped looking at the royal family (who seemed over-dressed, as always, in unsuitable clothes) and could hardly take its eyes off *la jeune francaise*.

The match itself was no walk-over for the comparatively-inexperienced French youngster. Indeed, the first set went to 10–8, after fluctuations of fortune (with Mlle. Lenglen in the lead 4–1 at one point – later reaching set point at 5–3 – and Mrs Chambers nearly there at 6–5 at another) before the French girl won through. Her returns from the net to the champion's backhand had been mainly responsible for giving Suzanne the set, but the Englishwoman had been playing strongly throughout, with her deep-driving passing shots particularly effective and noteworthy.

Again, in the second set, fortunes swung back and forth, before Mrs Chambers succeeded in levelling the match when she won through, 6–4. Emulating the champagne-swigging Norman Brookes, Suzanne Lenglen again drew gasps from the crowd when she had brandy from a neat flask her father offered her at this stage in the match. Clearly refreshed, she reached a 4–1 lead in the deciding set, only for the defending champion to struggle grimly back until she held two match points against the French challenger, at 6–5 and 40–15, to the almost delirious plaudits of the capacity crowd. Volleying brilliantly and leaping characteristically high to save apparently impossible-to-reach lobs, Mlle. Lenglen kept her nerve and asserted her superiority in stroke play, to win the set by 9–7 and the match by two sets to one, so giving notice of her take-over bid for world leadership in ladies' lawn tennis which was to succeed so splendidly in the years to come. In fact, although it was not known at the time, Mlle. Suzanne Lenglen was to play in the championships at Wimbledon six times, and would never be beaten, although bad luck was to dog her in every case, in that she would be faced with the worst draw possible on every appearance.

But what a crowd-puller the tempestuous and sophisticated Suzanne became. Before long, all her singles matches at Wimbledon had to be played on the Centre Court, because no other court could possibly cope with the crowds that always attended her progress to the final.

Of her first astonishing meeting, much earlier, with the girl who so convincingly took over from her as queen at Wimbledon, Mrs Lambert Chambers was to tell later, in a broadcast, in these words:

'I was reigning World Champion when I first heard the name Lenglen. It was 1914 and, at 15, she was already the talk of the south of France. My friend, Sir Arthur Balfour, warned me of her on the eve of a visit I was making to the Riviera to play in a tournament. 'If you let this child prodigy beat you,' he said, wagging a finger at me, 'we shall not allow you back to England!'

'In the Nice tournament, we were drawn in opposite halves, as it happened, so that we did inevitably meet in the final. Suzanne's father, who had made her what she was, closely studied all my matches, and even umpired some of them, which was a bit un-nerving, I can tell you. I went on court for the final feeling very nervous indeed, for the good and simple reason that I felt deeply that it would be humiliating for the champion of the world to be defeated by a mere schoolgirl!

'In the event, I won fairly easily in two straight sets, but I was very much impressed by the knowledge of the game the child possessed already, and I was quite sure that she would be a great tennis player one day.'

Recalling later events, Mrs Chambers went on: 'I was unable to play competitive tennis during the 1914–1918 war, whereas Suzanne was luckier during the period, in that she continued to be coached by her father and given practice by the leading French men players. Anyway, in those days the champion stood out, not playing in the competition, but in waiting for the winner to come through. This had its advantages, as well as its dis-advantages, but I think it is right that the champion should play through the competition.

'I was giving Suzanne a good many years when, as reigning champion, I faced her in 1919. I don't believe in excuses. You play, and you either win or you lose. But there were certain *facts* on that occasion that undoubtedly contributed to my defeat.

'I was lady champion in name mainly, as there had been no championship since 1914 and I had scarcely played at all since then. Granted, I was able to practise briefly on the Centre Court for my clash with Suzanne, but it is not the same thing as playing before the crowded stands – an experience my opponent was meanwhile becoming well used to as she played through the fortnight.

'Then, when my challenge day arrived, and I was ready, dressed and waiting to be summoned to the Centre Court, what should happen but a sudden downpouring of rain. The tarpaulin was quickly brought into use, but we had to wait for the rain to cease altogether before play could begin. I don't think I have ever spent a more miserable afternoon, and the more so as we were confined more or less to the dressing-room, and could only prowl around by the hour, getting more worried and fussed

every moment. It was late in the day before the decision was
taken to abandon the match and play it the next day instead.
By then I was quite a bundle of nerves. So I certainly did not
feel my best the next day, although I believe I played my best in
the circumstances.

'In those days, the Secretary of the All-England Club always
umpired the match, and famous men players gathered on the
lines. I feel these were appropriately gallant gestures which
should not have been allowed to pass out of Wimbledon traditions. The crowd loved the gallantry as well as the players, and
the staging added to the sense of occasion. Anyway, in 1919, in
addition to King George V, Queen Mary and Princess Mary, the
Australian Prime Minister, Mr Hughes, was present, as were
Lord Curzon, Admiral Beatty, and many other notable people.
There was also the biggest crowd I had ever seen at Wimbledon,
many of whom had slept out all night to get places.

'The Saturday, in contrast to the Friday, was a perfect day
for lawn tennis and for me. I detest wind and was relieved to
find there was only the lightest of light ones. And, although the
sun was shining, the heat was bearable, thanks to occasional
clouds. The court grass was in absolutely perfect condition, as
usual, which was just splendid, because I always played my best
tennis on the immaculate turves of the Centre Court.

'I got my confidence back fairly quickly after I had won the
first game to love. But there were many strenuous rallies in the
first set, and it was only after a terrific struggle, in which I was
forced into the peak of my play, that I conceded it to Suzanne
by 10–8. She seemed to wilt for a time in the second set, while
I was still strong, but she somehow pulled out reserves of strength
and played me closer than my 6–4 success would suggest. After
an interval, in which she drank some brandy and I was glad of
the rest, we resumed. I felt cold in the third set and could have
done with a stimulant myself, except that such a thing was not
English. I played badly for a time and Suzanne went on 4–1.
Although she was in luck with some net-cord strokes, I fought
back to 4–4. Unfortunately, by this stage in the match, I was
footsore and weary, having run many miles after her cleverly-
placed balls. I was also becoming mentally tired. By five-all,
the crowd was worked up into a state of intense excitement and
became even more so when, after a very long game of rallies, I

reached 6–5 and 40–15, with two points for the game, set and match.

'Alas, it was not to be. Clinching the winning point had been a nightmare to me all my playing life. I also lost my concentration, in thoughts of how the newspapers, which had strongly backed Suzanne, would have to climb down, which was foolish. Anyway, the rest is history. I threw away the vital game and she went on to beat me 9–7 in that set, so winning the match, 10–8, 4–6, 9–7.

'A message came from the Royal Box with His Majesty's congratulations to both of us. We were invited to visit the Royal Box but were too exhausted. Later, the King told me he had felt quite ill when the match reached crisis point! That made at least two of us!'

Mrs Lambert Chambers was to have a chance to gain her revenge in the following summer, when she easily won the all-comers' championship and faced Suzanne, as the new holder, in the challenge final. But Mlle. Lenglen was improving all the time and made no mistake in demolishing the Englishwoman's counter-challenge in two sets 6–3 and 6–0.

Afterwards, Mrs Chambers said: 'In my view, Suzanne stands alone as supreme world champion. She has mastery of every stroke, complete control of the ball, and uncanny anticipation.' This was praise indeed.

It was in 1920 too, that the American invasion began to bite at Wimbledon, at least as far as the men were concerned. Previously, their greatest success had been to win, through Maurice McLoughlin, the all-comers in 1913. Now they had a two-pronged leadership in the reigning champion, W. M. 'Little Bill' Johnston and his young rival, W. T. 'Big Bill' Tilden.

Part of the reason for the sudden American break-through in 1920 undoubtedly was that the First World War had not halted tennis in the States, as it had in Europe, but it was also due to the fact that a crop of fine young players was maturing there, as had been happening in Australia before the war.

Johnston, the much-respected nine-stone favourite, was well below par in 1920, unbeknown to the betting public, and went out somewhat ignominiously in the second round (albeit in four sets) to the Irish rugby and tennis international player, J. C. Parke. William Tatem Tilden, on the other hand, was improving with every match he played, and was destined, indeed, to take the American championship from Johnston that year, having previously fallen victim to him in 1919. Anyway, Tilden had little difficulty in disposing of Parke in the next round at Wimbledon, although he found it less easy to account for Britain's best singles player of the post-war era, A. R. F. Kingscote, in a fine five-setter in the quarter finals.

By now, Tilden's timing of his topspin backhand, which he had been working to perfect for years (to add to his always-considerable and beautifully co-ordinated range of strokes) was bang on, and by using this stroke for solid defence as well as for driving attack, he was shaping up as the most formidable of men players ever, with his powerful service, plus strong baseline driving, on forehand or backhand. He played all-court tennis which, alas, would go out with Kramer two decades later, and would never quite be repeated to this day, except possibly by Rosewall.

Tilden became something of a god at Wimbledon, as much because he treated tennis as a science and worked at it professionally, with self-criticism, every day and in every way, as through his dynamic, forceful 'winning' personality. He also studied his opponents whenever he had the opportunity, and sought out their weaknesses in order to exploit them. Indeed, more than any other early player, he pushed the game forward into the 20th century and set new standards for orthodoxy in the Eastern style, to the point that Rod Laver is on record as quoting his coach, Charles Hollis, to the effect that 'in a sense we are all Tilden's disciples'.

There were other ways in which Tilden was standard bearer for today's professionals. A natural crowd-puller, he deliberately set out to attract ever-larger followings for financial reasons; and he was the most temperamental of players in the eyes of referees and linesmen.

Anyway, while Tilden had been forcing his domination on the Wimbledon singles challengers in his half of the draw, a surprising outsider had been ploughing through parallel matches to meet up with him in the final of the all-comers. He was the Japanese champion, Z. Shimizu. However, 'Japanese Joe' failed in the role of giant-killer. The tiny Eastern stylist had promised more than he could deliver, and the 6 feet 2 inch 'Big Bill'

Tilden k.o.'d him in three straight sets, mainly by slowing down to play a restrained game (a precursor of his coming reputation as the greatest-ever exponent of controlled speed in tennis) with his slicing a match-winning feature.

Then came the real final. It was fantastic – an American-Australian clash for the first (but certainly not the last) time at Wimbledon, with the U.S. challenger slightly odds-on to win. Reigning champion Gerald Patterson was still a fine player, but he now lacked the finesse of the crowd's new favourite, Bill Tilden.

Like Lenglen, who was his only real rival for the affections of the Wimbledon crowds, and with whom he had much in common in terms of fast, sparkling all-court play, Tilden was not lacking in sartorial showmanship. His wardrobe included a furry white sweater which hung loosely almost to his knees and gave him the look of a fabled yeti from the Himalayas, or a Canadian grizzly bear. He was blessed, too, with the physique of a Greek god, and the stir among the maidens when he walked, grinning sardonically and bowing confidently, on to the Centre Court for the final against Patterson was something new altogether. Wimbledon had welcomed its first pop hero, as it were.

By contrast, Gerald Patterson was a fighter to whom finessing was less important than giving the maximum in strength and power. His smash, for instance, was rated the most formidable in tennis for almost a decade. Equally tall, he was of even heavier build than Big Bill Tilden, with the shoulders of a lumberjack and the jutting jib-like jaw of a man-o-war. He had attained admirable adaptability by playing the Australian circuits, which consisted of mixed-quality grasscourts and hardcourts constructed of loam, gravel, asphalt and other miscellaneous materials, the main demand on which was that they should be really hard and fast in proportion to the heavy rolling that went into their preparation.

Patterson, who had promised at the age of 19 to be one of the toughest competitors of all time, had lost a bit of his robust strength during the war years, when he had served as an officer in the trenches of France and Flanders, gaining a Military Cross in the process. He had, nevertheless, won the singles at Wimbledon in 1919, at the age of 24, in convincing fashion, and was relying now on his fantastically powerful service (allied to his strong net work) to 'ace' and volley Tilden, two years his senior, out of the championships.

The meeting of the monarchs of the Australian and American glens, at Wimbledon in May 1920, appeared to start badly for the favourite, who lost the first set to Patterson 2–6. But, in truth, Tilden had been probing and needling the Australian to find his Achilles' heel. As 'Big Bill' had heard, and as he suspected in the first few games, Patterson had occasional trouble with his footwork when going for a backhand shot and was therefore inconsistent in returns from the backhand.

This was all Tilden needed to know. He bombarded the champion's weak flank from then on, using a heavily-sliced shot which found its mark, to Patterson's discomfiture, again and again. Down went the holder, in four sets, 2–6, 6–2, 6–3, 6–4, and Wimbledon had found one of the greatest of its all-time champions in William Tatum Tilden.

Meanwhile, the other new Centre Court darling, Suzanne Lenglen, rapidly becoming the complete mistress of her craft, and set fair to be judged the finest woman player of all time, was again crushing Mrs Lambert Chambers in the 1920 final, as already mentioned, in straight sets, 6–3, 6–0. Her increasing grace, as she waltzed and strode through the championship match, commanded awe in everyone who watched her, reminding de-votees of a trained dancer as much as of a tennis champion, with her leaps, long strides, precise timing and perfect balance, all executed with verve, style and dazzling speed.

Lawn tennis had become a marvellous amalgam of sport, entertainment and 'religion'. Its shrine at Wimbledon was ablaze with light, excitement, good news and financial rewards which more than justified the faith of the founding fathers; but they had understandably erred in allowing for but modest expansion over the years. The ground in Worple Road was too small for the 'twenties, and the spectator arrangements were far too cramped.

So it was that, just after the Wimbledon fortnight in 1920, an agreement was signed between the Lawn Tennis Association and the All-England Club that the latter should purchase a larger ground in Wimbledon to suit the exigencies of the world cham-pionship and the increasing prestige therefrom. The fact that some of the courts at Worple Road had adjoined the old District

Railway on which trains steamed noisily from Southfields to East Putney, had not gone down well with some modern-minded foreign officials.

Henry Wilson Fox, M.P., who was then president at Wimbledon, and who had done much to keep the club in reasonable shape during the war years, was a leading light in steering the move, which (when he was forced to retire through ill-health in 1921) would be ably followed through on by his successor, Sir Herbert Wilberforce.

Anyway, after much searching, the apparently-ideal ground had been found in 1920 in Church Road, Wimbledon (ensuring the continuance of the lawn tennis name with the Mecca-like magic) and one of the leading architects of the day, Stanley Peach, had been appointed to oversee its fabled construction, which was expected to take at least two years to complete.

Church Road was then only a cart track, off Wimbledon Park Road, with farmland and farm buildings facing the new club location. A footpath, where Somerset Road now is, led to a delightful right-of-way known as Dairymaid's Walk. But the site's big advantage was that it adjoined the other two great treasures of the area – Wimbledon Cricket Club and Wimbledon Park Golf Club.

Part of the reason for the long period between the site being acquired and the transfer being effected was that the most careful and complex arrangements were made to dig and prepare foundations which would ensure perfect drainage conditions under the turves for 'the best courts in the world'. One of the attractions of the Church Road site had been that there was a lake fairly near at hand, and the herring-bone drainage system was laid in such a way that all water found its way to the lake which was in fact, located in the heart of the golf course.

A water tower was also created to produce a reserve supply for watering the lawns in the event of a mains fault or a drought. Perfectionism was still the aim of the All-England committee responsible. The water was pumped to the tower from the golf course lake, whence the fall would give enough pressure for a good spray from the hosepipes.

The country was searched for the finest possible turves for the new ground, and these were found at Silloth, Cumberland. The chosen greensward was made up of what is known as sea-washed turf, and there were stories that it was found to be full of live shrimps. The turves had to be boxed before they were laid, to ensure uniform thickness.

Meanwhile, as unprecedented demands from players and spectators for entry and for seats continued, a period of patch, make-do, mend, and temporarily-enlarge had to be embarked upon at the ageing original ground.

Bill Tilden was back on the Centre Court, and he was now at his brilliant best, in May, 1921, when the last championships were held at Worple Road. This time the rival finalist was an outstanding young personality from South Africa, Brian Norton. The entry for the men's events had been far and away the greatest in the history of lawn tennis, and B. I. C. Norton had astonished everyone by reaching the challenge round final, after surviving gruelling five-setters against America's F. T. Hunter and Spain's Manuel Alonso.

A complete individualist, a rebel, a mercurial, but not to say irresponsible, high-liver, Norton was a firefly on court, always on his toes and fast as lightning in his movements. Fair-haired and pixie-like, with a wicked smile, Norton's stroke play was elegant as it was attractive, and over the 14 days of Wimbledon he built a popular following almost as great as that of the champion.

Their 1921 final was therefore a fantastic crowd-puller. There were stories of tickets changing hands for twelve times their face value and of youngsters camping out for days to be at the head of the queue. Most of these enthusiasts believed that the All-England Club would say farewell to Worple Road with a new young champion enshrined in its trophies, for the very good reason that Tilden had only recently left a nursing home and was scarcely fit. It was less than a surprise, therefore, when Norton won the first two sets, 6–4, 6–2, and looked ready to take three in a row. But the prophets had reckoned without the South African's odd temperament. Upset apparently by the way in which some of his supporters in the crowd were barracking Tilden's drop shots, 'Boy' Norton (so called because of his schoolboyish antics on court) eased up and apparently chose to allow the American to coast through the third and fourth sets, 6–1, 6–0. It was one of the most amazing afternoons in the history of lawn tennis, and the crowd was bemused, as well as restlessly excited, as they tried to analyse what was going on.

In the final set, Norton appeared to be undecided whether to win (which, in view of Tilden's obvious fatigue, he seemed perfectly capable of doing) or whether to accede gracefully to his famous opponent. Indeed, when Norton was at 5–4 and 40–30, he still seemed in two minds, but at this point fate made the decision for him. He put up an easy ball for the champion and Tilden put it, as he thought, safely away. Instead it flashed on the line in a way that might have been in or out. Always sporting, Tilden assumed it to be out, and ran to the net to congratulate the new champion. But the linesman was insisting the ball was in and the umpire had to call 'Deuce'. Tilden then went on to win the set, 7–5, and the championship, against his unpredictable opponent.

In the last year of the original Wimbledon, the ladies' singles also attracted crowds that threatened to cause the collapse of the condemned Worple Road premises in the proverbial pack-of-cards manner. Once more and for her hat-trick, Suzanne Lenglen sailed into history, when she defeated the talented Miss Elizabeth Ryan by the convincing margin of 6–2 and 6–0, and it was not inappropriate, perhaps, that the last ball to be hit by a tennis racket at the old Wimbledon was propelled by the Frenchwoman who was probably the greatest lady player of all time.

Chapter Four / The best-laid Plans

The first few months of 1922 were incredibly hectic at Church Road, Wimbledon, the more so as the spring advanced and the date of the first tournament drew ever closer. While an army of carpenters worked desperately to complete the large new stands in time, furious preparation proceeded aimed at turning the carefully-laid grass patches into lawns fit for the world's best lawn tennis courts. The Cumberland grass, which was at least six inches long by now, had to be carefully mown to billiard-table smoothness, and this proved no easy task. Simultaneously, an application of wood ash was spread over it, and hand-weeding was begun. Between 50 and 60 teenaged youths, under a grounds-man, were employed ridding the courts of their main weeds, which were sea pink and thrift, and of any strange grasses which might have crept in. They used six-inch-long weeders, specially made from bits of reinforcing steel left over from the frame-works of the stands, with a sharp point at one end and a loop at the other. Rolling followed, using a two-ton monster, pulled by a team of men, with the backbreaking work being done both lengthways and crossways. By one of those delightful bits of forgetfulness that give a place character, some behind-the-scenes architectural planner forgot to leave an opening on the drawings for the heavy rollers to be taken out when the stands were built around them, so that they had to remain there in full public view for as long as the stands remained as they were – a coveted viewing position for the ground staff and their friends.

The new Centre Court was, of course, given special attention and the news was released to the press that it was in such good condition shortly before the 'fortnight' that it should prove to be 'the fastest lawn tennis court in the world'.

A week before the tournament, the stands were still echoing to hammering and the shouts of the foremen, but the courts were ready to the point that it was possible to cover the principal ones with tarpaulins (hoisted tent-like at nights) to ensure that they would play dry and fast.

But the best laid plans of field-mice and tennis men gang aft agley. The grass under the tarpaulins was in perfect condition for the 1922 tournament – not too wet and not too dry. But the English weather was in a particularly wayward mood that year. The first Wimbledon fortnight at the new Church Road ground was opened on 26 June by the King to the accompaniment of a downpour of rain, and thereafter it continued as the wettest two weeks Wimbledon had ever experienced. Indeed, as far as can be ascertained, there was never a wetter Wimbledon – not even the Jubilee tournament in 1926, which was bad enough by all accounts.

Day after day, in the 1922 championships, the vast tarpaulins, each one weighing several tons, were manhandled off the courts, only to have to be laboriously replaced several times before evening. The first round of the men's singles were seriously delayed; outside courts were wet or unplayably soft and spongy for most of the second week. Tilden, who had cut his finger badly, had chosen not to appear, so that the prospects for the final of the men's singles for the championship of the world was that much less exciting. Nevertheless, the entry had proved once more to be a record one, and the public turned up in its thousands, little daunted by the deluge. King George V and Queen Mary were as enthusiastic as any and, despite the weather, attended Wimbledon half-a-dozen times during the fortnight.

The L.T.A. and the All-England Club had at last arranged for the challenge round to be abolished in all events so that the rule was that the champions had to play through for the first time at Wimbledon in 1922 – a rule players had been trying to have introduced for years. Alas, the draw for the championships would not be seeded yet awhile – not until 1927, in fact.

In fact, this affected only one event. Mlle. Suzanne Lenglen was the only holder competing in 1922.

The opening match on the new fast Centre Court was appropriately a singles one between two British players – the 'top seed', as it were, A. R. F. Kingscote, and a comparative rabbit, L. A. Godfree. In virtue of the fact that he served the first ball on the great new Centre Court, Godfree was allowed to keep it as an historic souvenir.

Kingscote went on to take the Australian champion, G. L. Patterson (the recognised master of the service ace and of the smash) to five gruelling sets before being knocked out of the tournament. Before going on to regain the singles title he had last held in 1919, Patterson also had a tough semi-final battle with his power-driving compatriot, J. O. Anderson (whose christian name was James, but who was always known by his initials). J. O. had perhaps the strongest forehand in the game at that time and knew how to use it to maximum advantage. He was to become Australian champion three times, but would never win the Wimbledon singles.

Patterson and Anderson met many times over the years and their clashes were always occasions of magic and of thrills. Their styles were opposite – Patterson aggressive and hot; Anderson calculating and cool – but they seemed to interlock into absorbing sequences of power-play and all-court play by turns. On this occasion, in 1922, they certainly gave value for money, with Patterson concentrating characteristically on service and net attacks, while Anderson played his accustomed speedy baseline game. In the course of a five-hour match on the Saturday afternoon of the second week (the men's singles having suffered severe delays due to the rain) they offered little quarter, the one to the other. In the end, Patterson won through, 6–1, 3–6, 7–9, 6–1, 6–3 in five incredible and gruelling give-and take sets. By comparison, the final, in which Patterson defeated Randolf Lycett (also an Australian, but now masquerading as an Englishman) by 6–3, 6–4, 6–2, was tame and dull.

But perhaps the greatest happenings in the men's singles that year were there to be seen by intuitive observers of young talent. No fewer than three future champions were in the lists, every one showing remarkable promise, and all of them Frenchmen. They were Jean Borotra, René Lacoste and Henri Cochet, each just 17 years of age – three of the fabled 'four musketeers' of the later 'twenties.

1922 was not a great year for the famous female compatriot of the three teenagers, Suzanne Lenglen. In playing through the tournament for the first time, she seemed to lose something of her magic, temporarily at least, being taken to vantage games both by Miss McKane and Miss Ryan before facing the new American champion, Mrs M. Mallory, for the world championship before a capacity attendance. Their finals' match had been delayed by the weather and by the fact that the five-set marathon men's semi-final between Patterson and Anderson was running on and on. Although it was seven in the evening before the exhausted Aussies came off the court, Mlle. Lenglen refused to have her match postponed, and her American opponent went along with her in this. Suzanne was keyed up to play that night, and play she did, k.o.'ing Mrs Mallory in only 25 minutes, by 6–2, 6–0. Suzanne went on to become a triple winner in that year, when she won the mixed doubles with Pat O'Hara Wood, of Australia, and the ladies' doubles with Miss Ryan.

The first Church Road championship also saw the longest doubles fight on record up to that time, when H. Roper Barrett and B. I. C. Norton came five times within a point of beating the champions, Patterson and O'Hara Wood, before going down 15–13 in the fifth set! The latter pair were so exhausted, they went out in the final to Randolf Lycett (G.B.) and Anderson at 11–9, again in the fifth set.

At the end of the 1922 championships at the great new ground at Church Road, Wimbledon, everyone was delighted with the success of the fortnight in every department, with the probable exception of the ground staff, who, with their part-time assistants, had laboured through a nightmare of signals to cover and uncover courts at high speed, as many as five or six times a day, with covers weighing as much as five tons each.

America took over from Australia again in the men's singles at the new Wimbledon's second year in 1923, when 'Little Bill' Johnston 'came right' and went quickly through the card, defeating Norton in the semi-final by 6–4, 6–2, 6–4 and compatriot Frank Hunter in the final, 6–0, 6–3, 6–1, having lost only one set altogether in the course of playing through. It was a popular victory, with the crowd's only regret being that the match lasted only 45 minutes, due chiefly to Johnston's fantastic topspin forehand drive, his volleys and his sliced service, all of which had matured at the same time, as had his weight control and his timing. 'Big Bill' Tilden considered 'Little Bill' Johnston to be the greatest sportsman in lawn tennis, and the Wimbledon crowds concurred. The unassuming little man, so small in stature and yet so big in heart, was undoubtedly one of the all-time favourite winners at Wimbledon.

Another up-and-coming champion-to-be had joined in the fray, and had fallen to Bill Johnston early on. This was Vincent Richards, then 19 (while Johnston was 28), who had been discovered by Bill Tilden in Yonkers when he was 13, and who had an astounding, prodigious natural talent for the game. Tilden, by the way, was absent from Wimbledon in 1923 for the very good reason that he had had to have the top joint of the middle finger of his right hand amputated as a result of the accident, previously mentioned, which had kept him away in 1922. Perfectionist as always, Tilden was, at the time of the Wimbledon fortnight, finding a way to modify his grip and overcome the loss by eliminating the weakness. He was able to do this by elongating his 'full eastern' style forehand grip so that the thumb (as seen from the front) was more or less in line with the stump of the damaged middle finger, instead of between the tips of the index and middle fingers as heretofore. He was to claim later that the new grip style actually improved his play, but this is as may be. He was probably improving fast at the time anyway.

Suzanne Lenglen, meanwhile, was setting hearts a-fluttering, female as well as male, as she resumed her unbeatable, all-conquering game, and as she showed off the latest in French sports fashions, topped as always by colourful bandeaux. In the course of the 12 sets she had to play in six matches, to win the 1923 title, Suzanne lost only 11 games, and she was able to assert her authority to such an extent that she coasted through most matches, in minutes rather than hours, from the centre area of the baseline without ever advancing to the net.

1923 was also the year of 'the babes'. They were two bonnie teen-aged English 'roses', Joan Austin (a sister of the equally talented Bunny Austin) and Evelyn Colyer (daughter of a well-known dental surgeon, Sir Frank Colyer). Somehow, to the delight of the Wimbledon crowds, 'the babes' reached the final of the ladies' doubles, where they faced Mlle. Lenglen and Miss Ryan, who were seeking their fifth championship doubles' title. The 'babes' were excellent volleyers and attractive stroke players. Alas, their nerves were bad for the first half hour or so, and the large crowd was disappointed to find the scoreline going to 4–0 in favour of the champions. But there was fun to come from the two youngsters who so obviously enjoyed their game and their partnership. By an inspired volleying attack, Joan and Evelyn took three games in a row from the 'veterans' and came within a point of making the score 4–4. That was their big moment. The reigning champions overcame their shock, pulled ahead to win the first set 6–3, and then took the second one by 6–1. But Britain had had a moment or two of uninhibited joy in the midst of the mainly-foreign successes, and 'the babes' were the talk of the town that week.

In 1924 the famous agreement was signed, between the Lawn Tennis Association and the All-England Club, which made the L.T.A. joint-owner of Wimbledon with the founding club, and under which the association assumed full financial responsibility for the tournaments held there. The world championship had been abandoned as such, although the Wimbledon titles were still regarded as the premier ones by all concerned.

It was a time of change and advancement. The rights to make the rules of the game of lawn tennis had also been handed over by the L.T.A. to the International Lawn Tennis Federation, with the fascinating proviso that they should always be printed in the English language.

Except for the ladies' singles, which the Incomparable Suzanne had now made her own, France had fared rather badly at Wimbledon in its first 48 years, to the chagrin of a race who still believed that tennis had been their national game from the Middle Ages onward, and that Britain had virtually stolen the prestige and the kudos. But things were now swinging France's way with a vengeance. Pride had dictated, since the French National championship had been introduced in 1891, that no foreigner could become champion of France. This had undoubtedly held back the advancement of French players' standards of play for a time (and continued to do so until the rule was changed in 1925) but gradually her youngsters had been becoming 'blooded' on the courts of the world outside France. Decugis and Gobert had made their marks to some extent on the pre-Kaiser-war tennis scene, but it was the arrival on the Wimbledon courts of the 'four musketeers' of tennis that ushered in what became known as 'the French era' at Wimbledon – the six years, from 1924, when Frenchmen dominated the grass courts tournaments; the years when Borotra, Lacoste and Cochet (who made up the four, with Brugnon) each won the Wimbledon singles championship twice (although none of them won it twice in a row!); the years when only Frenchmen would appear in the final of the singles championship, with the exception of 1926, when Howard Kinsey of America faced Borotra, and lost to him, on the famous Centre Court. The fourth musketeer, Jacques Brugnon, was better as a doubles player than in singles matches.

Jean Borotra it was who first broke the Anglo-Saxon male dominance at Wimbledon, when he reached the final and won the championship in 1924. This was the year the All-England Club and the L.T.A. had chosen to introduce a modified form of seeding to the draw, aimed at separating the nominated players of any one of the twenty countries participating (not exceeding four in number) as widely as possible, so that there would be a negligible chance of their meeting.

Unofficially that year, the world's top seed (and therefore Wimbledon's) was Tilden, with his protegé, Vincent Richards, rated number two. With 'Big Bill' unable to take part, all eyes in 1924 were on young Richards, but he was not yet ready to parry the accurate net attacks of Jean Borotra, to whom he went out in the second round, after winning the first set.

The Bounding Basque, as beret-wearing Borotra was known, flew through to the final, thanks to his tactical exploitation and his acrobatic technique of getting to the net and volleying accurately on even the slightest chance. His opponent, René Lacoste, a much less extroverted human being, had had a tougher fight in reaching the first-ever all-French final. In particular, Manuel Alonso, the polished Spaniard, had made him fight for five gruelling sets in the second round (and had led for a time by two sets to one). Lacoste, the youngest of the Musketeers, could have been the greatest, except for ill-health which dogged most of his career, to the point that he more or less chose to retire from top-class competitive tennis in 1929, at the age of 24, after six short but great years in the spotlight. His backhand was reckoned to be the best ever seen on a tennis court, and his other great strength was a rock-like baseline defence.

Lacoste had not quite fulfilled his promise by 1924, however, and his friend Borotra was able to dictate the pace of the match by dominating the net and preventing any inclination to long defensive rallies. The result of this was that the match turned out to be the shortest five-setter in lawn tennis history, the score in Borotra's favour being 6–1, 3–6, 6–1, 3–6, 6–4. It was a popular victory. The Bounding Basque had quickly established himself as a glamorous and heroic figure with the crowd – the D'Artagnan of the Four Musketeers and the very personification of *la belle France* in all his explosive elegance.

Lacost, who sought to be a personality in his own right by wearing a white peaked cap (in contrast to Borotra's black beret) was basically an introvert and a serious young man, so he could never be accepted quite so warmly. Respect, rather than affection, came to be lavished on him by the English fans.

Among the other notable events of the 1924 fortnight had been the astonishing come-back registed by Australia's veteran, Norman Brookes, the 'master' who had claimed the first of his two world lawn tennis crowns as long ago as 1907.

Brookes, at 47, had faced 30-year-old Wimbledon runner-up, F. T. Hunter, of America, in the third round and had won through astonishingly in five sets. This match, perhaps more than any other, helped to establish Brookes as one of the greats of all time.

And the other noteworthy occasion in the 1924 championships was the launching at Wimbledon of the new young American ladies champion, an 18-year-old dynamo, Helen Wills, who, as Helen Wills Moodie would be the first and only woman player to surpass the Wimbledon achievements of the 'Incomparable' Suzanne. Alas, she did not meet Suzanne Lenglen in the final, as everyone who knew the form was hoping. The dynamic Miss Wills reached the ultimate stage all right, but Mlle. Lenglen, suffering from exhaustion following an attack of jaundice, had meanwhile scratched from all events, on doctor's orders, subsequent to beating Miss Ryan in a splendid quarter-final (after losing her first-ever set at Wimbledon, in five years of top-class play).

Astonishingly, the final unexpectedly but gloriously brought its moment of triumph to the top-ranked English girl, Kitty McKane, when she became the first native Wimbledon champion since the war. Her defeat of Miss Wills was well-deserved, but some luck was involved as it was patently secured against the run of play. Miss Wills also got her name on the roll of honour for the first of many times when, in partnership with Mrs Wightman (who was to give her name to the cup of that name) she convincingly won the ladies' doubles.

In the following year, 1925, with France continuing to dominate the scene, the controversial qualifying competitions were held, prior to the Wimbledon fortnight, at the Roehampton Club. This 'screening' procedure had been introduced primarily because more and more players from many countries had been complaining year after year that it was unfair when their entries for the greatest of all tournaments had not been accepted. But instead of simply solving a problem, the altered rules created a new one of apparently equal proportions. Instead of the cries of previous moaners, a new volume of noisy complaints began at once to build up, from players who had been made to qualify and felt they were above that sort of thing. But, in the main, it was agreed that the qualifying competition was a good thing, and should stay.

Three out of the last four in the men's singles in 1925 were Musketeers – Borotra, Cochet and Lacoste – resulting in the same final line-up as 1924, with the result neatly reversed, Lacoste beating Borotra, the holder, by 6–3, 6–3, 4–6, 8–6. Lacoste had learned his lesson and saw to it this time that Borotra did not dominate the match from the net, and, in the much longer period the disputed four-setter took, he was able to establish his iron rule on the play. It was a notable and much enjoyed victory by the 'outsider' in the betting stakes.

Meanwhile, in the ladies' singles, the 'female companion' in the Dumas plot, Suzanne Lenglen, happily recovered from her illness, was playing perhaps the finest tennis ever offered up by a woman at Wimbledon, in the course of setting up the fantastic all-time record of playing through to the final and winning the championship for a total loss of only five games (winning forty games in succession, by the way) and beating the reigning champion, Miss McKane, en route, to the tune of 6–0, 6–0 – a record which has never since been equalled and certainly never can be beaten. Alas, although no one knew it at the time, this was to be, in essence, the Incomparable Suzanne's swan song at Wimbledon.

Chapter Five / Faites vos jeux Monsieurs, Mesdames . . .

The All-England Club celebrated its lawn tennis Golden Jubilee in 1926, commemorating fifty years of championships at Wimbledon, albeit at two different locations in the town. Inevitably, it was a right royal occasion, with the King and Queen in the Royal Box and their son, the Duke of York (later to be King George VI) taking part in the tournament, partnered by his Equerry, Wing-Commander Sir Louis Greig, in the men's doubles.

On the opening day of the fortnight, all the surviving champions who could make their way to Wimbledon by any means, from wheelchair to aeroplane, were lined up on the centre court to receive commemorative medals from the hands of King George V and Queen Mary. The ex-champions were led by the man who had won the second Wimbledon tournament, in 1878, P. F. Hadow, and by the first lady champion, Miss Maud Watson, so it was quite a turn-out. Curiously, although the men wore lounge suits, many of the famous ladies wore their tennis dresses, headbands, bandeaux and the like. There were even some who (ignoring the modern ideas introduced by Mlle. Lenglen) still wore suspender belts, long woolly stockings and the other unsuitable impedimenta of early tennis styles, under their ankle-length sports dresses! Conversations, as they waited in line for the royal party to arrive, were certainly animated, helped by the fact that some of them were meeting for the first time in over forty years; the chatter was also punctuated by shrieks of disbelief and sighs deep out of memory; as this went on, the packed crowds in the stands were happily playing 'spot the winner' as they relished the pleasures of nostalgia.

The Duke of York, who played left-handed and would be rated a worthy club competitor even today, was unfortunate to be drawn in the doubles against the highly-seeded ex-champions, A. W. Gore and H. Roper Barrett, and did not win a set. Nevertheless, a good time was had by all, in this history-making event, and not least by the large, respectful 'ooh-aahing' crowd, who had never dreamed of seeing the King's son grace so relatively humble a court.

But the true royalty of Wimbledon were still the likely winners of the men's and ladies' singles.

In one of the most thrilling semi-finals staged in the fifty years of tournaments, Jean Borotra was taken to five sets in the men's singles by fellow-Musketeer, the strong-willed but small-in-stature stylist, Henri Cochet. Their different styles found point and counterpoint on this occasion in a match that had the colourful and knowledgeable crowd gasping almost with disbelief at the length of the rallies and the variety of the strokes being exhibited. Cochet, who was perhaps the greatest of the four Frenchmen, could almost always beat the beret-bedecked Borotra on hard courts, but the Bounding Basque usually had a slight edge on grass, which he barely managed to demonstrate in this match (as the scoreline of 2–6, 7–5, 2–6, 6–3, 7–5, shows). But win he did in the end, before going on to a popular Jubilee championship win in the final.

Borotra, Tilden and Lenglen were the truly-great tennis stars of the time and by far the finest crowd-pullers in the game. As Borotra triumphed in 1926, Tilden was regrettably absent from Jubilee Wimbledon, and Mlle. Suzanne Lenglen was equally-regrettably present for only part of the fortnight, in traumatic circumstances that could have served as an 'unlikely' plot for any of the Hollywood 'ruined by success' epics of the period.

Suzanne was the greatest. She had been so superior to the so-called opposition in her six Centre Court singles victories that it was rare for a game to be taken off her, and only one set was so taken over the years of her queenship at Wimbledon. But serious temperamental tantrums had been taking over her personality from about the time that substantial offers were being made for her to turn professional – offers which had become much more insistant since she had beaten her successor-to-be Helen Wills, 6–3 and 8–6, in their only encounter at the Carlton tournament in Cannes in February, 1926 – three months before the Jubilee event at Wimbledon, at which Miss Wills was unable to be present.

Curtain-up on the sad drama began on the Wednesday of the first week of the fortnight, when Queen Mary made the journey to Wimbledon especially to see the queen of the Centre Court. Suzanne was scheduled to play a ladies' doubles match at 4.30 that afternoon and a singles match was quickly arranged for 2 p.m. so that the Queen of England could have full value for money. Suzanne was later to claim that she did not know of the single because she had not been told. Be that as it may, she did not turn up at the royal-graced ground until 3.30. This was bad enough, but as soon as she reached the dressing-room, she gave vent to a display of temper, refused to change into her tennis outfit, and demanded that the double should be played first, whatever the desires of Queen Mary and her attendant officials might be, and she added that the single could be played another day. This did not go down well with officials already at boiling point over the unscheduled delays and the royal box anxieties. There were some hot words, as a result of which Suzanne marched off to her hotel declaring that she was in-different whether she played or not, but that if the matches *were* rearranged for the next day it was imperative that the double should precede the single. Surprisingly, this was agreed to, Queen Mary having to be disappointed in the process – an event over which much displeasure was evinced from Buckingham Palace.

Such a thing probably would not have been done for any other player in the world, and certainly the championships should be greater than any champion, but so popular was she by now that the tempestuous and quixotic Suzanne got her way. The rules were bent. Other players were leaned upon to adjust schedules and there were stories that one woman had to choose to drop out of the tournament altogether in the interests of the fixtures. Some-thing of this unhappy state of affairs was inevitably felt by the pub-lic, who, for the first time, exhibited displeasure towards their idol – presumably considering the honour of the British Queen to be greater than the pride of the French 'queen'. Thereupon Suzanne got moody and played only in half the matches scheduled over the next several days. Inevitably, as a result of all the tensions and happiness, her asthma returned, and she chose to retire

Players of the 1880s. Back row, l.-r.: E. de S. H. Browne, Rev. J. T. Hartley,
C. W. Grinstead, Miss Maud Watson, H. F. Lawford, W. Renshaw. Seated:
E. Renshaw and Miss L. Watson

W. Renshaw *v.* H. F. Lawford in Fifth Wimbledon Singles Match

Lawn tennis at Wimbledon in 1895

Top left: America's May Sutton (later Mrs Bundy). *Left:* Fashions of 1914. *Above:* 'Laurie' Doherty, with 'snowshoe' racket. *Below:* Strawberries for tea?

Above: Mlle. Lenglen and Miss K. McKane. *Below:* Bill Tilden in action, 1929

Top left: Miss Joan Fry playing Miss Helen Jacobs, 1927. *Top right:* Miss Helen Jacobs, a Wimbledon favourite. *Bottom:* Miss Helen Wills followed Mlle. Lenglen as fashion queen

Left: An overnight queue for admission in the late '30s. *Below:* King George V and Queen Mary were keen spectators

Spectators, including two chauffeurs, who didn't get inside!

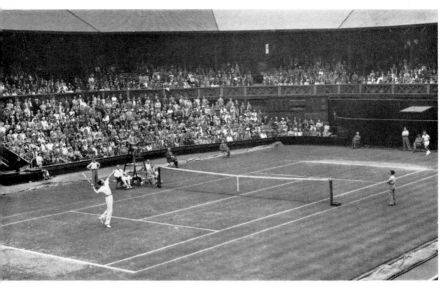

Baron von Cramm *v.* D. M. Grant at Centre Court

Damage by German bombs, October 1940

Miss Maureen 'Little Mo' Connolly in 1953

Rod Laver the magnificent

Miss Louise Brough, Big Game player in the Ladies' matches

Left: Big Jack Kramer. *Right:* Lew Hoad. Favourite power-players of post-war Wimbledon

Miss Althea Gibson—first non-white
player to triumph at Wimbledon

1961—Miss Angela Mortimer with
the Trophy

'Pancho' Gonzales at the first 'Open'

1970—Ken Rosewall in play against
Roger Taylor

1969 Open—Miss Ann Jones slumps in pain on the Centre Court

1970—Mrs Margaret Court in the Ladies' Singles Final

1964—Miss M. E. Bueno receives the Trophy from Princess Marina

1962—Miss Billie-Jean Moffitt, delighted at winning the Final

Players of the 70s. *Right:* Roger Taylor, Britain's No. 1 of 1971. *Centre:* Australia's young prodigy, Miss Evonne Goolagong. *Bottom:* Hard-hitting champion John Newcombe

from the singles at once. It was then only a matter of time before she scratched from the rest of the tournament, to the despair of officials and the deep disappointment of her fans.

It was the year before seeding was introduced to the draw for the ladies' events and, to be fair to Suzanne (who was still highly-strung as well as asthmatic) luck had ordained that all the top players were in her section of the draw. She was also torn by advice from hangers-on, and she dithered and stormed. And she made the mistake of withdrawing from the greatest tournament in its most glorious year, when still at her peak. It was a decision that she was to regret all her life.

The still Incomparable Suzanne (who has never been equalled for sheer dominance of the tennis scene allied to almost fanatical crowd support) again made a terrible mistake when she turned professional, later in 1926, wooed by manufacturers, in the new world as well as the old, to use their goods and services in public and to endorse them in advertisements. The 'daring ma'm'selle of tennis' (whose calf-length dresses and knee-length hose had already caused a bigger stir in their time than mini-skirts and hot pants in a much later era) helped to thrust Patou into modern circles, as far as clothes were concerned, and did much for a range of business houses in cosmetics, perfumes, chapeaux, shoes, jewellery, sportswear, tennis equipment . . . and bandeaux, this last being still and always her trade-mark: the redeeming halo above the hawk-like, last-of-the-Mohicans nose.

But professionalism did not suit the first lady of tennis. All this frantic commercial activity was concentrated into one short year (in which she made a commercially successful but temperament-destroying tour of America).

During this multi-match processional circus, Suzanne some-how managed to show that her game was still well-nigh perfect in all departments and that her early dance-training had made her the most graceful and beautiful mover ever seen on a tennis court in the States. But twelve months were more than enough. Early in 1928, she set up the Lenglen School of Tennis in Paris, in which city she died, on 4 July, 1938, at the age of only 38. It was reported that she found happiness in the end. If so, the Incomparable Mlle. Suzanne Lenglen undoubtedly earned and deserved it. She was 'the greatest'.

Alas, the only encounter Suzanne had with her almost equally-

C

great successor, Helen Wills, was the one already reported on hard-courts in France. They never met on grass (and never at Wimbledon), so the arguments will go on and on, and will perhaps even be fed into computers, to decide which girl would have won, had they played in ideal circumstances.

Certainly, if personality is taken into account, Suzanne (with all her faults) *was* supreme. As an artist she was a natural high-flier. Yet she also had that rarest of qualities, the common touch – the ability to be regarded as a goddess by the public, while also being accepted as 'one of them'.

By contrast, Helen Wills (later to be Mrs Wills-Moody, and later still Mrs Roark) was the almost-perfect tennis machine. Suzanne, with her brandy breaks, her Gallic shrieks and her Pavlova leaps after impossible balls, could attract capacity crowds even when she was steam-rollering the opposition. Helen's pre-dictable victories were less well-attended.

'I regard her as the coldest, most self-centred, most ruthless champion ever known to tennis' – this was the opinion of Big Bill Tilden, writing about Helen Wills in his autobiography. These 'killer' qualities were certainly to pay off, in that she would surpass Suzanne's record by winning Wimbledon eight times (albeit over a longer period), but there is no doubt that there was less magic around her, and that she is remembered with much less affection than the French girl.

Helen Wills won the first of her eight Wimbledon titles in fine style in 1927, when she beat the talented by tem-peramental Spaniard, Señorita Lili de Alvarez in the final. Apart from this important event, 1927 was undoubtedly one of the vintage years of Wimbledon, with four brilliant world champions listed in the men's singles draw in the persons of Borotra (the holder), Tilden, Lacoste and Cochet, and with the astonishing true-to-form 'happening' of all four meeting in the semi-final, with both matches going to five sets before Borotra and Cochet were just able to break through to the final. The entertainment value matched the stature, the more so as the four had such different styles of play. Tilden, the all-stroke player; Borotra the great volleyer; Lacoste the baseliner; and little Cochet the master of the all-court game.

1927 was, coincidentally, the year of the complete seeding of the draws in all events, and it certainly seemed to be working well, despite unpleasantly wet weather for a second year running. Another important milestone of the year at Wimbledon had been the retirement of Commander G. W. Hillyard, who had been All-England Club secretary for almost 20 years. He had been followed by Dudley Larcombe, husband of the former ladies' champion and manager of the Roehampton Club, who was in turn to hold the post for almost 14 years.

The return of Bill Tilden to Wimbledon, with his sixth American Championship under his belt, was a big bonus for the club in terms of record crowds. Big Bill was in peak form, and, when he met the apparently-nonchalent Henri Cochet in the semi-final, he soon won the first two sets, 6–2, 6–4, and was leading 5–1 in the third set when Cochet somehow suddenly succeeded in winning the dominance he had sought against the American from the start. In truth, they were well matched, and each had won once in their previous two encounters. Cochet of the iron will fought back brilliantly from the gateway to failure (at 1–5 in the third set). Relentlessly, he won that one, and the next two, to clinch the match and face his compatriot and friend, Jean Borotra, in what promised to be a great great final. Both Borotra and Lacoste had already become Wimbledon champions. Cochet, the brilliant little giant from Lyons, felt that, in 1927, it should be his turn at last. An ex-ballboy, and a natural tennis player, he had been involved in the game, one way and another, from the age of five.

It was indeed a memorable final in the event. Astonishingly, Cochet again quickly found himself behind by two sets. This time, with his nerves of steel, he equally-convincingly won the next two, to reinforce his title of Five Set Cochet. The ultimate set, with Cochet playing his usual tight-rope-walking game, was a joy to all who saw it. In the main, his all-court tactics were the perfect answer (so rarely seen) to Borotra's high-powered volleying. But normally Borotra was unbeatable if he was allowed (as he was on this occasion) to net-rush his way to a position of consistent attack at the start of the final set. A sustained onslaught took the trail-blazing Basque to 5–2 and to match point no fewer than six times before the score was levelled at 5–5. The imperturbable Cochet had saved all six points in a phlegmatic but secure style the Wimbledon crowds had never seen in 51 years. With his perfect timing, his marvellous smash, his strong forehand and his incisive volleying, the lion-hearted Cochet then paced himself to winning the set at 7–5 and the match with it, by 4–6, 4–6, 6–3, 6–4, 7–5. The ovation the tiny Frenchman received at the end was one of the warmest ever to spread across the Centre Court.

In the ladies' singles, the green eye-shielded Helen Wills had slickly caught the crown Suzanne Lenglen had so unhappily dropped. No more beautiful than any of her predecessors, and apparently much less human, her clinical attitude to the game and its consequences tended to set the Centre Court crowds against her. This was more true in 1927 when she faced Lili de Alvarez, the colourful, wayward and often-brilliant Spanish champion, who was also probably the most beautiful of the top tennis players of the decade. It was a one-sided final, but the soon-prejudiced crowd made a heroic loser out of Señorita Alvarez and drew from her some thrilling responses in tactics and strokes. In particular, she delighted the spectators by hitting out freely and fearlessly at any half-volley that was offered, from any position on the court. Attack and attack again became the Latin's hot-blooded ploy, and it made for a spectacular final in the face of Helen Wills' glacial play. In the end, Miss Wills won by 6–2 and 6–4, but it was the Catalan runner-up who got the loudest applause from the knowledgeable crowd.

By contrast to 1927 and its excitements, 1928 offered a disappointingly dull fortnight – this despite the fact that Patterson had joined the four ex-champions (Tilden, Borotra, Cochet and Lacoste) in contesting the singles title. The holder, Cochet, again reached the final (with Tilden just managing to prevent an all-French semi-final) faced this time by Lacoste, but was off-form and went down in four rather poor sets to give his fellow-countryman his second victory. The only real interest for talent-spotters in 1927 had been earlier in the contest when a fresh-faced English youngster, W. H. 'Bunny' Austin, had taken Lacoste to five sets in knightly fashion. The ladies' singles had been a somewhat colourless re-run of the previous one, with Miss Wills this time beating a below-par Señorita Alvarez by 6–2, 6–3.

Bunny Austin 'came good' quickly in the following year, 1929 – despite surprisingly being unseeded – to reach the semi-finals of the men's singles, the first Britisher to do so for six years; not only that, but he then took Jean Borotra (in their first encounter) to four sets, 6–1, 10–8, 5–7, 6–1, before the Basque again went on to meet Cochet (who had brilliantly disposed of Tilden in straight sets, 6–4, 6–1, 7–5, in the other semi-final) in a repeat of their previous Wimbledon final, with Cochet gaining his second big win, more comfortably, by 6–4, 6–3, 6–4.

Although the fact was not realised at the time, this was the end of an era: the French epoque. The dominance of the Four Musketeers had lasted for six years, 1924–29, during which time three of them, Cochet, Borotra and Lacoste, had each won the singles championship twice, although none had won it twice in succession, the roll of honour having read: Borotra, Lacoste, Borotra, Cochet, Lacoste, and Cochet. The mild-mannered, shy Jacques 'Toto' Brugnon, the fourth and the eldest Musketeer, never won the singles title for the very good reason that he was the great doubles' specialist of the group, always ready and able to partner any of the other three and bring out the best in them as far as the doubles game was concerned. In all, he won the Wimbledon doubles four times, twice each with Cochet and Borotra and also appeared in three other Centre Court finals.

Eleven years separated their birth-dates, which ranged from 1895 to 1905, but they had all arrived on the Wimbledon scene and established their personalities, with their talents, in 1923, when their 'mother comrade', Suzanne Lenglen, was already there to greet and guide them. Collectively, three of the four equalled Suzanne's Wimbledon singles record by totalling six championships, as well as providing five runners-up. And, when the men's doubles were taken into account, their incredible tally was ten wins.

Following Cochet's masterly 1929 victory over Borotra, no French player reached the final at Wimbledon for seventeen long years – until Yvon Petra succeeded in the singles in 1946 – although Borotra and Brugnon did break the gap by winning the doubles twice, in 1932 and 1933.

Chapter Six / Champagne Perry and vintage Vines

Although unemployment was soaring to unmanageable levels and poverty in the north of England was a scandal, the 'twenties ended with Wimbledon unchanged in its slightly snobbish isolation from the real world. The attendances were as remarkable as ever, and the coveted pleasure of tea on the lawns of the members' enclosure remained one of the most desirable summer outings for aspiring social climbers, with strawberries, iced cakes, cream buns, cucumber sandwiches and other 'pinkie up' delights available to the few in abundance.

W. T. Tilden was smarting somewhat from the eclipse he had been suffering at the hands of the French. He had reached the semi-final at Wimbledon in 1929, before going down to Cochet, but although it was apparent to the discerning that he was now past his best, Big Bill would not admit it, and being third or fourth best in the world was not good enough for his continuing perfectionist aspirations. And he was right when nearly everyone else was wrong.

In 1930, against all the odds, he made a spectacular come-back at Wimbledon. In the semi-finals, while Cochet was being vanquished by the hard-hitting W. L. Anderson, Tilden was overcoming Borotra in a memorable five-setter. The two Americans then faced each other on the Centre Court on the final day of the fortnight, and Wilmer Anderson was forced into a three-set defeat that left him in no doubt that, at his best, Bill Tilden was the greatest. Happier than he had been for years, Tilden then turned professional, never to be seen playing in the Wimbledon championships again. He was sadly missed at Church Road, for he had been one of the great characters of the decade.

1931 was an impoverished year at Wimbledon as far as top talent was concerned, Tilden having turned professional and Cochet, badly out of condition, due to go out in the first round to Britain's Nigel Sharpe. It was the end of a long period (broken only by the First World War) in which star names had always been drawn to compete for and win the world's greatest prize at Wimbledon. Indeed, 1931 brought the first walk-over in the men's singles since the challenge round had been abolished, when Frank Shields (America) retired, with an injured leg muscle, in favour of his fellow-countryman, the sandy-haired Sidney Wood. Wood's only difficult match had been against a raw teenager, Fred Perry by name (with Wood having to struggle to win by 4–6, 6–2, 6–4, 6–2), while Shield's hardest match had been the semi-final one against a fading Borotra. Disappointingly for Britain, her most talented tennis son of the day, Bunny Austin, had led Shields by two sets to one in the quarter-final (and thereafter by 5–4, 40–30 and match point) but somehow had lacked the killer finish (as was always to be his weakness) and had eventually gone out, 6–3, 2–6, 5–7, 7–5, 6–1. This was tragic, in a way, because Austin easily beat both Shields and Wood a few weeks later in Paris. But then, as is common knowledge, Austin was in the mould of 'great British losers' and would find his name in the histories of the game as possibly the best native player never to win Wimbledon.

Another player who had everything going for him in 1931 except the will to win was the stroke-master Jiro Satoh of Japan. He could have been another Cochet had his determination been stronger.

Fred Perry, who had scored a sensational win over J. van Ryn (America) in the quarter-final, before going out in the semi, was made of altogether tougher stuff and was recognised in 1931 as the likely more-successful successor to Austin.

Wood, who won through in this disappointing year, thanks largely to a phenomenally-fast service, was, at 19, the youngest player ever to become Wimbledon champion – or half-champion, as he rated himself when Shields withdrew.

In the women's singles, too, a not-quite-star-quality player took the championship, in the tiny shape of Cilly Aussem (in an historic all-German final in which she beat H. Krahwinkel), Helen Wills-Moody having been unable to make the trip from the States, and the second favourite Señorita Alvarez, having been beaten by a 21-year-old, Dudley-born Sunday-schoolteacher, Dorothy Round. There was further hope for future English successes in the inspired play of two 18-year-olds, Peggy Scriven and Betty Nuthall, who both reached the last eight, and in the promise shown by 17-year-old Kay Stammers who took four games off the experienced Dorothy Round in the first round.

It was soon clear that Britain's excellent male and female prospects still could not quite reach their years of fulfilment by 1932, and Americans more or less carved it up between them once more. Helen Wills-Moody had returned to Wimbledon, and she easily regained the ladies' singles title 6–3, 6–1 (in an all-American final against the other up-and-coming Helen – Jacobs by surname) losing only thirteen games in the twelve sets she played in the competition.

In the even-more-glamorous world of the men's singles, a great new star name had been telegraphed from the States – that of H. Ellsworth Vines, a 20-year-old Californian, who was reigning American champion (having more or less swept the board in the States for two seasons already) and his arrival at Wimbledon was greeted by scenes of enthusiasm and studious interest in complete contrast to the comparative lethargy of 1931. Here, by all accounts, was a great new talent – brash, bold and gangling – expressed in the frame of a true son of the New World: handsome as a film star and walking tall like a young god.

Speed and power were the keynotes to the strong, coltish Ellsworth Vines's game, and in both respects he was superior to any tennis player who had gone before, not excluding the great Bill Tilden. The trajectory of the balls he hit on the forehand was astonishing, thanks to the flatness of his strokes, and it was his main regret that he was less strong on the backhand. His service, too, thanks to his great height and reach, and to the degree of wrist-snap his Emerson-type grip allowed him, was of the rocketing-cannonball variety, with little need for spin. His lobs were also hard and straight, and some were said to have bounced violently into the royal box, to the consternation of the occupants.

This was the man whom Wimbledon saw for the first time in 1932, and it was no surprise that the crowds soon began to follow him from court to court. With the looks and charm of a Gary Cooper, plus the fire and power of a young gaucho warrior, it is little wonder that he was rated a worthy successor to Big Bill Tilden.

Cochet, who had been made number one seed, on a basis of known form, played waywardly (as he was inclined to do betimes) and was put out of the tournament in only the second round by a Scottish doubles player, I. G. Collins. Good sport that he was, Cochet immediately entered for the consolation singles competition, known as the All-England Plate (open to anyone knocked out in the first or second round of the competition proper) and won it in double-quick time. This was an important landmark for Wimbledon. Up to that time no famous player had ever entered the Plate Stakes; his sportsmanship showed what could and should be done, and the prestige of the event was immediately boosted, to remain so for many years.

Satoh, meanwhile, had k.o.'d Collins and Sidney Wood (the holder) only to be beaten himself in the semi-final by Bunny Austin, while in the other half of the draw, Vines had disposed with ease of his alleged rival in the power-game, the Spaniard, Enrique Maier, in the quarter-final, and had destroyed the redoubtable Australian, Jack Crawford, in the semi in half-an-hour, for the loss of only six games. Cochet, the spectator, was provoked to declare: 'C'est magnifique! Wimbledon has never seen anything like it.'

Bunny Austin (cheered to the skies as the first Englishman to reach the singles' final for ten years) had his chance to make history on the Centre Court on the last Saturday of the 1932 fortnight, but Vines was too much for him – so much so that the Englishman admitted afterwards that he had been unable to see some of his opponent's crushing aces, let alone return them, and he was steadily demoralised. The tell-tale score-line read: 6–4, 6–2, 6–0, the last set taking only ten minutes. The score-card afterwards revealed that the incredible Californian power-hitter had put away 30 aces in his 12 service games, winning the match with the final one.

In becoming champion, incidentally, Ellsworth Vines had established the astonishing record of losing only 19 games in the last three rounds of the championship – a record that would stand for 15 years before finally being beaten by Jack Kramer.

Again, to almost everyone's surprise, not one of Britain's great young prospects, male or female, was able to pull off a title in 1933 at Wimbledon, although Dorothy Round managed to give Helen Wills-Moody a bit of a fright in the ladies' singles final before the King and Queen, no less, plus King Feisal of Iraq, the Princess Arthur of Connaught, Princess Ingrid of Sweden and other notables. The other British achievement was Bunny Austin's 'first', when, to the consternation of the tennis establishment he appeared on the Centre Court in shorts.

The men's final, a repeat match between the somewhat lazy but brilliant Australian, number two seed, Jack Crawford, who always rose to an occasion, and the younger but over-exposed American, number one seed, Ellsworth Vines, was nevertheless rated by many (including S. A. E. Hickson, umpire at the very first Wimbledon and an observer at every final up to and including this one in 1933) the finest final, in the classic mould, in the first 56 years of Wimbledon lawn tennis championships. An epic five-set struggle in which Crawford, the baseline-playing defender, established the rhythm, and Vines, of the concussive service and attacking volleys, the power, resulted astonishingly in the younger man being exhausted earlier, and in the immaculate and uncomplicated gamester, Crawford, turning from defence to attack to win – against all the betting – by 4–6, 11–9, 6–2, 2–6, 6–4. No cheers were louder from the packed assembly around the Centre Court than those of Queen Mary, who had long nursed a special affectionate admiration for the tall and powerful Australian.

Alas, Vines was to turn professional soon after this, and would never play at Wimbledon again, but in the two years he held the centre of the amateur lawn tennis stage, he was undoubtedly one of the greatest performers of all time. A measure of his sportsman's eye and of the strength of his arms was that after drawing record gates as a tennis 'pro' (while beating Tilden, and later Cochet, and later still, Perry) he moved on to golf and at once found himself in the big money there, too.

Gentleman Jack Crawford, on the other hand, was to cause other sensations at Wimbledon, and was to go on entertaining the tennis crowds until well into his fifties – the steady, reliable, calm, wristy, English-styled player, whose good-natured tolerance was legendary, and who always inspired faithful, affectionate support. His 'old-fashioned' classic style was widely copied, particularly in Australia, where he was to win a total of eleven national titles and countless State championships, and where his impact pushed tennis forward ahead of its time, and set standards many of the world's greatest players would follow therefrom.

After exactly a quarter-of-a-century of eclipse in the Wimbledon singles, Britain came into her own in 1934 and won both titles convincingly. There are those who say we would never have made it that year had it not been for 'Wimbledon throat', but it is my belief that Britain would have triumphed in 1934, whatever the odds, with our top players maturing simultaneously and their supporters carrying them to victory on a wave of patriotic goodwill.

Wimbledon 'throat' was a virus of some sort that hit several top players, including the reigning champion, Jack Crawford, and forced half-a-dozen miscellaneous challengers to retire. But Crawford was fit by the time he reached the final and faced Britain's greatest player of the quarter-century, Frederick John Perry, the Lancashire-born and London-raised 'natural' of lawn tennis. The self-taught Perry was seeded number two to Crawford, and the others in the top list were the great new German hope, von Cramm, at three, followed in order of seeding by Austin, Shields, Stoefen, Wood and de Stefani.

Perry had been a world champion table-tennis player before entering the lawn tennis spotlight, and his style of play in the latter owed much to his experience and experiments in the former. Tall dark and handsome, Fred Perry made a name for himself, in three short years, from 1934, that would echo down the decades until it is still a household word today, as that of a shrewd businessman as well as in the remembered accounts of past glories in the annals of popular sport.

Perry reached the singles final in 1934 via a gruelling see-sawing five-setter in the semi-final against Sidney Wood, which he won 6–3, 3–6, 7–5, 5–7, 6–3, while Jack Crawford was having just as tough a match in his semi with Frank Shields, which ran out 2–6, 4–6, 6–4, 6–3, 6–4. The final was a great one for Britain and for Perry. The weather was perfect and the presence of half-a-dozen members of the royal family in the box beside the Centre Court gave a sense of occasion to the proceedings.

Although Fearsome Fred seemed to start badly, and was soon 1–3 down in the first set, he was, in truth, weighing up Crawford and figuring how he could best hustle the phlegmatic big Australian out of his masterly game of patient, disciplined accuracy. That he quickly found the answer was soon echoed in the roars of the crowd (enjoying a new experience for English followers of sport) as Perry astonishingly won 12 games in a row, in the now-famous run which took him from 1–3 down in the first to 1–0 up in the third. The 6–0 centre set was one of the few times Crawford had ever lost a set to love, and it was due to Perry's policy of all-out attack, featuring his fantastic speed in returning service and getting to the net (in the best Wilding manner) that the Australian was jolted out of his usual game of well-placed-and-timed passing shots. The final scoreline of 6–3, 6–0, 7–5 established Fred Perry as a worthy world champion of lawn tennis, as well as of table tennis, and as a great national hero – so un-English in his flamboyant aggression, his will-to-win, and his showmanship, and yet so English in his sportsmanship, his good taste and the generosity of his open-handed approach to each game.

Before the men's final, the ladies of G.B. had been re-writing the record book, too, to the delirium of their previously-frustrated supporters. The absence that year of Mrs Wills-Moody was undoubtedly a contributing factor to the fact that Dudley-born Miss Dorothy Round faced Miss Helen Jacobs in the final of the singles, but the way in which she disposed of the brilliant young American left no doubts that England had once more produced a lady player of world class. The score was 6–2, 5–7, 6–3 and, although she was modest in bearing, there was an incisive quality about the play of the Midlands' schoolteacher and Sunday-schoolteacher (who always adamantly refused to play on the Sabbath) that showed the character of the true champion.

Miss Round, whose classic stroke play was a joy to watch, had had hard matches in the quarter-final (against Mlle L. Payot of Switzerland) and in the semi-final, when she was strongly challenged by the greatly-experienced Mme. Mathieu. But her resilience was remarkable, and in the all-important final match on the Centre Court, against Helen Jacobs, she wisely played an attacking, volleying game. The match eventually turned on the seventh game of the third and final set, when Miss Jacobs was leading 3–2 and had a point in hand to make it 4–2. Instead, Miss Round made it 3–3 and so moved into the vital seventh game with a chance. It was here, in a desperately fought-out struggle, that Durable Dorothy showed the iron in her backbone by relentlessly wearing down the American, while tirelessly chasing after even the least likely of balls, until she had made it 4–3. That was it. The other two games for the 6–3 set were never in doubt, and as Miss Dorothy Round was presented to the King and Queen, British hearts beat faster and the applause around the Centre Court had never been louder. Miss Round (with R. Miki of Japan) also won the mixed doubles, so it was altogether quite an English renaissance after so many years spent by home players in the deep grass among the 'rabbits'.

Not only had an English rebirth taken place in 1934, but also a whole new spirit had entered into lawn tennis via its Wimbledon shrine; for five years (until the outbreak of another world war once more suspended the tournaments) it was the sport of princes, and of the fittest men and women of their day; it offered superlative competitive entertainment, and a whole range of godlike gentlemen of the courts, including Perry, Budge, von Cramm, Riggs and Kramer, who set hearts a-fluttering over the years.

In 1935, Fred Perry, the Englishman, became the first man to win the main event at Wimbledon twice running since the challenge round had been abolished. The seeds this time, from one to eight, were Perry, von Cramm, Crawford, Austin, Allison, Wood, Menzel and Boussus. Appropriately, the first two seeds faced each other in the final, and Perry proved, beyond question, that he was the master of the driving forehand that was von Cramm's forte.

That was fine. But there had been an astonishing upset earlier, when an unseeded and relatively unnoticed youngster had put out two seeded players (plus the talented but unseeded Adrian Quist, of Australia) to reach the semi-final, no less. His name was Donald Budge; he was red-haired; and he had developed a phenomenal back-hand while playing baseball in his native California. Now, at 19, he had put out Quist in straight sets, Boussus in four sets (including a 6–0 score in Budge's favour in the final set) and Bunny Austin by 3–6, 10–8, 6–4 and 7–5. Clearly, although von Cramm overcame him by 4–6, 6–4, 6–3, 6–2 in the semi, Budge was obviously a future champion-in-the-making. And there were *two* good teenaged prospects, for all who had eyes to see, in the 1935 lists, not just one. The other was Vivian McGrath, of Australia, who, barely 18, had k.o.'d number five seed, Wilmer Allison in the first round, using a double-handed technique never exposed at Wimbledon before. McGrath was a sensation, in the same way that Budge was. Alas, he would not fulfil his promise to anything like the same extent.

The great match of 1935 – a fine year in all departments – was probably the final of the ladies' singles between America's two Helens. They had met before on the Centre Court, in the 1929 final, when the then Helen Wills had massacred Helen Jacobs by 6–1, 6–2. That the namesakes, both from Berkeley, California, did not like one another was well established by now, there having been a famous incident, in the U.S. final in 1933, when Miss Jacobs had sought to sympathise with an injured Mrs Moody, only to be snubbed. So it seemed likely that the 1935 final would be a needle match, to put it mildly.

In the event, there *was* another near-sensation in the third set, when it was one set all and Miss Jacobs was leading 5–3, with a match point in hand. The icy Mrs Wills-Moody had not been faced with defeat like this since she was 18, in 1924. But although it seemed to the 14,000 spectators, most of them seeking her blood, that Helen Wills-Moody had irretrievably lost the match to her less conventional rival, in fact her steady, orthodox game carried her though (after Helen Jacobs had volleyed away the vital point). Indeed, before winning the set at 7–5, and the match by 6–3, 3–6, 7–5, the imperturbable, fluent 'Queen Helen' (or the 'Venus with a headache', as Tilden cattily described her) would not yield, and never gave Helen Jacobs ('Brunnhilde with a shovel', in Tilden's equally sharp assessment) another chance, playing steel-nerved, copy-book strokes against the attempted stabs, chops and clever footwork of the younger Helen. It was Mrs Moody's seventh 'world championship title' no less, and there would be one more to come in due course.

England won the ladies' doubles in 1935, in the popular persons of Miss Kay Stammers and Miss Freda James; Miss Round teamed up with Fred Perry to retain her mixed doubles' title; and with Fearless Fred taking the singles once more, Britain astonishingly recorded, in the 59th year of the championships, the total of three victories, with the Empire (through Australia) taking a fourth, the men's doubles, when Crawford and Quist astonishingly beat van Ryn and Allison, in one of the most thrilling finals on record.

England's peak year in this period of stirring renaissance, however, was undoubtedly 1936, when home players won every Wimbledon event except the ladies' singles; but no individual match was particularly memorable.

Perry now completed his hat-trick of Wimbledon singles' victories – the first man to do so since playing through was introduced for champions. Again, his opponent was Baron Gottfried von Cramm, the tall Aryan Adonis of sport in the 'thirties, who was a first-rate stylist with an unhurried technique which enhanced his 'gentlemanly' front. Von Cramm had defeated Crawford and Austin on the way, and the final was expected to be one of the greatest ever seen on the Centre Court (the more so as von Cramm had recently defeated Perry for the French championship). Certainly the first game, which involved ten deuces before Perry won through on service, promised a great match, but a pulled ligament tamed the German soon afterwards, so that Perry's 6–1, 6–1, 6–0 victory became somewhat hollow.

Meanwhile, to complete the almost clean sweep for the U.K. of four victories out of five, C. R. D. Tuckey and G. P. Hughes had won the men's doubles for Britain; Miss Stammers and Miss James had retained their ladies' doubles; and Dorothy Round, with Fred Perry, had done likewise in the mixed doubles, Miss Round for the third year in succession.

This time, in the absence of her Californian namesake, Helen Jacobs achieved her heart's desire by defeating Fru Sperling and taking the Wimbledon ladies' singles with comparative ease at last, having previously been runner-up no less than four times.

Immediately after the 1936 Wimbledon fortnight, Fred Perry turned professional, defeated Ellsworth Vines in his professional debut in New York (and later at Wembley) and proceeded to carve out a unique niche for himself in society and in business in the States as well as at home.

Chapter Seven / The Liberation of the Ladies

Coronation year at Wimbledon saw some reshuffling of official positions and the retirement of several old-stagers who had served the game well but perhaps too long. If Wimbledon has had a fault over the decades it has been to favour 'establishment' figures in official capacities around the courts. They tended, and indeed still tend, to appear year after year for the honour rather than the pay; they are all-too-inclined to be as deaf as they are blind; and some have even been said to be prone to taking cat-naps during play.

Anyway, in 1937, Mr Hamilton Price took over as referee from Mr F. R. Burrow and not, some said, before time. Mr Burrow was then seventy years old, not liked by many of the new young players, and apparently disinclined to like them back, or to sympathise with their more modern athletic points of view. Astonishingly, as a statistician was to reveal in a Coronation year programme, Mr Burrow had refereed 18 Wimbledons altogether (three of them at the Worple Road ground) and had been responsible for putting no fewer than 8,000 matches into court in all. So perhaps there was a measure of truth in his opinion that he invariably knew best.

As far as players were concerned, 1937 was undoubtedly Donald Budge's year, although there were many who had hoped it would be von Cramm's. Anyway, when the two met at Wimbledon that year, not in the championship proper, but in the final of the Davis Cup, it was a clash of such intensity and spirit that (at least until Cliff Richey would meet Ken Rosewall face to face in an epic struggle at Wimbledon in 1971) it would be remembered as the greatest battle of tennis champions ever seen anywhere. Indeed Tilden was to give as his opinion afterwards that the world would never enjoy a finer match.

Donald Budge had grown up in a family in which 'fitba' was all the talk. His father, 'Ginger' Budge, had played league soccer in Scotland as a professional, before emigrating to Oakland, California, to become a laundry manager, so the young Donald knew more about Rangers and Celtic in his early schooldays than he did about baseball or American football, or tennis. After being taught the rudiments of the Association game by Budge senior, but finding no outlet for it on the west coast of America, red-haired Donald had turned to basketball as a left-hander in his early teens, and had only reluctantly caught the tennis bug from his elder brother, Lloyd, at the late-for-a-champion-to-be age of fifteen. By the time he was 21, however, Donald Budge had written his name large in the annals of tennis as the first man ever to win the grand slam of the four major championships – Wimbledon, American, French and Australian – in the same year (and the only one until Rod Laver equalled the triumph a quarter-of-a-century later). But this was yet to come. We are in 1937, with the young prodigy from Oakland still only 20.

In the Wimbledon championship von Cramm had repeated the sequence of the previous year in beating Crawford and Austin on the way to the final, but Donald Budge had justified his number one seeding by forcing the German into the number two position of runner-up for the third year in succession (by 6–3, 6–4, 6–2) and giving him the tag of 'always the best man, never the bridegroom' – a reputation which had also taken hold of the talented but even-less-fortunate Bunny Austin by now. Indeed, it would be Budge who put out Austin when the Englishman reached the Wimbledon final for the second time in the following year.

But, as has been mentioned, the greatest-ever Wimbledon final, in 1937, had nothing whatsoever to do with the championship fortnight; it was one of the added features the 300 or so members of the All-England Club enjoyed in those halcyon days of lawn tennis – a Davis Cup inter-zone final between the much-fancied American and German teams (the winner of which was expected, the British team having been greatly weakened by Perry having turned 'pro', to take the Cup).

The tie stood at two matches all, when Budge and von Cramm

stepped on to the Centre Court for the decider. As at that moment, Budge was the ideal of American youth, and the Aryan Baron was perhaps the most admired man in the world of tennis. Both were fantastically fit and sharp, on the day. Using his powerful forehand crosscourt drives to advantage in an all-out attack he launched from the first game, the German prised the first two sets from the American by the narrow margins of 8–6, 7–5, only to find that Budge had dug in, and had got his eye in so well that he returned the compliment in much more convincing fashion in the next two, at 6–4, 6–2. Von Cramm then quickly hauled himself to the peak of his stroke-making skills in the final set, and was soon leading by 4–1. But courage and initiative were finding point and counter-point in this marvellous Centre Court match, and it was no idle promise 21-year-old Donald Budge made to his non-playing captain, Walter Pate, as the two champions changed ends: 'Don't worry, skip, I'll beat him in the end!'

Beat him Budge did, astonishingly but convincingly. Raising his game to a greater peak than ever before, the red-haired young American took chance after chance, working to death his world-famous backhand in the process, and using his long legs and arms to reach apparently impossible passing shots from von Cramm. The final result of the greatest final was 8–6, 7–5, 4–6, 2–6, 8–6, and a week later (as expected) America beat Britain in the challenge round to regain the Davis Cup for the first time in a decade.

Britain was again in decline at Wimbledon by the summer of 1937, and won only one of the five championships, when Dorothy Round regained the ladies' singles title, having put out the champion, Helen Jacobs, in the quarter finals along the way. The final, in fact, was one in which the Midlands girl had to pull out all the stops against the hard-hitting Polish champion, Panna Jedzrejowska, to win out 6–2, 2–6, 7–5, in a grim but entertaining match.

It is slightly melancholy to look back upon, but 1937 (with the war clouds gathering, and Munich only a year away) produced an England-Germany semi-final that was a crowd-puller for reasons other than patriotic pride or the desire to see an 'enemy' done down. It was the battle of the also-rans, the clash of the runners-up – the match that could decide which was the better of the two 'best players never to win at Wimbledon'. To the vast crowd's disappointment, Baron Gottfried von Cramm was superior to H. W. 'Bunny' Austin on the day. The stylish gentlemanly Englishman went down to the stylish Prussian baron, 8–6, 6–3, 12–14, 6–1, but 28-year-old von Cramm was again no match for the all-conquering 21-year-old Donald Budge, and lost to him in three straight sets, 6–3, 6–4, 6–2, in the alas-predictable final, with von Cramm establishing some sort of 'record' as runner up for the third year in a row.

The following year, 1938 (the year in which all five major events at Wimbledon went to Americans) the tennis world was stunned to hear that the battling Baron would be absent from Church Road, having been charged, found guilty, and imprisoned for 12 months, under German Statute 165, which dealt with homosexual offences.

Released from gaol in time for Wimbledon in 1939, Gottfried von Cramm flew to London, entered the pre-Wimbledon London championships at Queen's Club, defeated America's great new hope, Robert Riggs (destined to be 1939 triple Wimbledon champion, Budge having turned professional) in the singles, won the men's doubles with John Olliff, and was made favourite for Wimbledon one week later. However, it was not to be; rightly or wrongly, von Cramm's great chance was denied him. His entry was refused without explanation.

Anyway, to get back to 1938, with his German rival in prison, 32-year-old Henry Wilfred Austin (Bunny to his friends and supporters) reached the final of the singles for the second time, only to suffer an even heavier defeat from Donald Budge than that which he had experienced in 1931 at the hands of Ellsworth Vines. Budge was at the height of his powers (and indeed was to be rated by shrewd judges of tennis the world's greatest player of all time) and, in addition to grand-slamming his way to the Wimbledon, Forest Hills, Australian and French championships, he was to become a winner of three championship events at Wimbledon for the second year running.

The 'Queen of the Thirties', Helen Wills-Moody, was back at Wimbledon in 1938, after being absent in 1936 and 1937. Although she was rated favourite by the bookmakers, most experts considered that she was past her best. After all, she was 32 (which was old for a woman in those days, but not for a man). Miss Helen H. Jacobs, her opponent in the final (as she had been in 1929, 1932 and 1935) was not yet 30, and 29 seemed *so* much younger than 32.

In the event, both girls played equally well; it was a breathlessly neck-and-neck race at 4–4 in the first set, and anybody's match. Then, as Miss Jacobs advanced on the net and Mrs Moody banged over a passing shot, an over-eager leap to intercept caused the younger girl to twist and fall, damaging an ankle already known to be weak. Alas, it was, to all intents and purposes, the end of the match. Everyone could see that Miss Jacobs was finished. So could Mrs Moody, but she was too single-minded, not to say coldly ruthless, to let it affect her in any way. She banged away with her fastest, hardest serves; she drove as well as she had ever done, on both wings; she continued to produce strokes of great variety; in short she showed no mercy to her wounded compatriot across the net.

Mrs Wightman and others then tried to get Miss Jacobs to scratch, so that she would be saved further pain and humiliation. But her attitude was: 'If *she* wants another victory so much, she can have it the hard way.'

There were good reasons for this reaction by Miss Jacobs. In the 1933 U.S. final, especially, she had been robbed of a positive victory when the positions had been reversed. On that occasion, Mrs Wills-Moody had injured her back to the point that when she was 0–3 down in the first set she had spoken to the umpire, and an announcement had been made that she was going to default – at which Helen Jacobs had put her hand on the other girl's shoulder and had said: 'Won't you rest a minute, Helen?' To this Mrs Moody had replied icily: 'Take that hand off my shoulder.'

Now, the reversed position was working out quite differently, to underscore the opposite personalities of the two women. Mrs Moody proceeded to take the eight games necessary to complete her eighth all-time record-breaking Wimbledon singles championship. The match was concluded in a sort of stunned silence from the crowd such as had never been felt at Wimbledon before.

The loathing in which the two girls appeared always to have held one another was in no way improved by this event. Again we have the sequel reported in Bill Tilden's not uncatty autobiography *My Story*, published in 1948:

'Helen Jacobs summed everything up for me the following day when she said: "You know, Bill, I don't mind her being a so-and-so, but I object to her being a stupid so-and-so. If she had only smiled when she shook hands at the end and said 'I'm glad you broke your damn leg' – or something like that, then no one would have known how she felt." '

Yet Mrs Helen Wills-Moody-Roark (as she was soon to become, in the peculiar way that Americans have of tying on married names to single ones with hyphens) is regarded by many as the greatest woman tennis player the world has ever seen.

1939 was altogether a remarkable year at Wimbledon. Budge having departed to the professional ranks; Bunny Austin having become involved with the time-consuming recruitment campaigns of Moral Rearmament; and von Cramm's entry having been blocked. The men's singles was wide open once more. Nor was there an out-and-out favourite in the women's ranks, with 'la belle Helene' gone for good, and her namesake rather in decline. As it happened, America had reserves of young talent coming up, and she once again swept the board by taking every title. It was, in fact, Bobby Riggs's and Alice Marble's year.

Riggs created something of a Wimbledon record by never losing a match there. This was for the very good reason that he only played one tournament at Wimbledon (the 1939 one) and won all three events open to men, without surrendering a set in any of the final matches, by the way. Similarly (although not on her only visit) Alice Marble took all three titles open to women.

Riggs was a supremely confident young man of 21 who was mainly a baseline player. So sure was he of himself in the year the war began that a few days before the Wimbledon fortnight, he backed himself heavily with a London bookmaker to win all three events, obtaining excellent odds on the basis of his defeat by von Cramm at Queen's Club the previous week. His Centre Court final against his fellow-American, Elwood Cook, in the singles (which he won in leisurely but steady fashion – 2–6, 8–6, 3–6, 6–3, 6–2 – a match in which not even the bookies had much hope from the start) was disappointing in quality, but the result had never really been in doubt. Largely on the strength of his triple Wimbledon crown, he followed the two previous champions, Perry and Budge, into the ranks of the professionals.

Californian, Alice Marble, the daughter of a lumberjack, had
as great stature as Riggs, in her way, or perhaps greater. A tall
and shapely, if muscular, blonde, she was a totally new
phenomenon at Wimbledon – an early manifestation of women's
lib; a lady who chose to play the Big Game (as it would come
to be called) like a man in the singles, and to offer a men's
doubles-type game in the ladies' doubles with her friend, from
Sharon, Massachusetts, the elfin Sarah Fabyan (who, as a most
successful junior, had been Sarah Palfrey, and who was later
still to be Sarah Palfrey-Fabyan-Cooke). In brief, these two were
the earliest pioneers of a new hard-hitting school of women tennis
players, among the prize pupils of which, in years to come, would
be Pauline Betz, Margaret du Pont, Louise Brough, Doris Hart,
Billie-Jean King and Margaret Court, to mention but a few.

Alice Marble had actually played as a run-getter for a men's
baseball team in the Pacific Coast League in San Francisco, in
her teens, and girls don't come much tougher than that, even in
America. She was following the latest male style in lawn tennis,
too – particularly the big serve and the sustained net attack –
meticulously carrying it out in every respect except scale. She
attributed her technique to the teaching skills of Miss Eleanor
'Teach' Tennant, who was later to do the same sort of thing – as
guardian, tutor, and adviser – for Maureen Connolly.

Alice Marble, skip-hatted and impressive, had beaten Helen
Jacobs in three sets, 4–6, 6–3, 6–2, to become American
champion for the first time in 1936 and had taken the title again
in 1938 (with the 1939 and 1940 U.S. championships also due
to fall into her lap, before she would turn professional for a
very large sum of money). Her Wimbledon success in 1939 (in
which she lost only two games in the last two rounds) was totally
convincing, and she would undoubtedly have won the triple
crown again the following year, had it not been for the war. She
went on to make a success as a cabaret vocalist as well as in
professional tennis, although Gloria Swanson was to say of Alice
Marble's singing: 'I like the quality of her voice, but her style
reminds me of the English actor who says "I love you" as if he
were asking for a cup of weak tea . . .'.

Chapter Eight / Bang-bash-wallop dents the Velvet Turves

The so-called Big Game (or Power Game, if you like, or Bang-bash-wallop-bang) had been emerging from the interwoven patterns of all-court, all-stroke and baseline techniques in the years just before the war as the only 'new' style of play to develop for several decades. But it was in 1946 that the Big Game began to be talked about in tones of awe or admiration.

On the outbreak of the Second World War, give or take a week or two, the staff at Wimbledon had melted away like a butter pat in the sun, leaving only the new groundsman, Edwin Fuller, and one part-time assistant to keep the vast sports complex in trim. Fortunately, Red Cross, Air Raid Precaution and National Fire Service units were quartered in the famous ground (which mainly saw out the period of hostilities as a Civil Defence centre) and over the years they helped with mowing, rolling and other maintenance work. The American Forces in Britain held an annual tournament at Wimbledon and contributed some petrol, in return, for the mowers and tractors. But Wimbledon had few moments of glory, even in its international exhibition matches, between 1939 and 1945, while Britain fought with its back to the wall and tennis was virtually a forgotten game. Indeed, sticks of German bombs straddled several of the 14 grass courts, while pigs and chickens scratched around the All-England outbuildings to help feed the local citizenry.

When Major D. R. Larcombe, the club secretary, died early in the war, a woman took over for the first time. She was Miss Nora Gordon Cleather, who had been his assistant for a decade or so, and who was now designated manager rather than secretary. After making her home in the clubhouse for some years, the better to supervise the tiny staff and the Civil Defence 'lodgers', Miss Cleather retired before the end of hostilities, and in 1945 Lieutenant-Colonel A. D. C. 'Duncan' Macauley took over as secretary, assisted by another of the astonishing number of 'characters' Wimbledon has attracted, a Miss Bumpus. Col. Macauley had been assistant referee to Mr Hamilton Price (now also dead) before the war and knew the ropes extremely well. He had taken over in enlightened fashion, at just the right time, from Frank R. Burrow, who had tended to over-regiment competitors. Duncan Macauley, who was to become quite a legend at Wimbledon in the post-war years, was ably assisted in re-establishing Wimbledon quickly after the war by a new referee, Captain A. K. Trower, a disabled ex-serviceman who was highly thought of around club tournaments.

The war had been shorter for the Americans, and tennis had never ceased there in the way that it had in the U.K. So, it was from the States, not unnaturally, that the post-war Big Game arrived at Wimbledon – mainly in the impressive shape of Big Jack Kramer. Opposing him were no English names of consequence, but among the Europeans who surfaced at Wimbledon in 1946 were Jaroslav Drobny of Czechoslovakia and Josef Asboth of Hungary, both of whom had made their debuts at the famous English ground as talented youngsters in 1939.

1945 had seen the finals at Wimbledon of a mammoth 'victory tournament' organised by the American Forces, having been played off in a dozen European countries, with the zone winners descending on the newly re-opened ground at Church Road. But none of the big names was apparent in the services at this stage, and the men's singles final was eventually won by an Englishman, Charles Hare, who happened to have been in America at the start of the war, and had joined the U.S. Army.

As the proposed date for the first post-war Wimbledon tournament approached in 1946, therefore, the seedings could not be guessed at with any accuracy, especially as players from no fewer than 32 nations had accepted invitations to take part. Of the 1939 champions, Alice Marble and Bobby Riggs had long been professionals; Britain's best pre-war players (such as the veteran Kay Stammers, now Mrs Menzies, and the most promising youngster Jean Nicholl; 26-year-old Tony Mottram and 24-year-old Geoff Paish) were sadly out of practice, having been out of tennis altogether for six long years – Mottram as a bomber pilot who gained the D.F.C.

In both ladies' and gentlemen's singles, America appeared to hold all the aces. Less disrupted by a comparatively short war and unaffected by bombing, her clubs had been able to build up an almost embarrassing superfluity of young talent, just as her championships had continued successfully throughout the war period.

Among brilliant young men who had forced their way to the fore between 1939 and 1945 were Jack Kramer, Gardnar Mulloy, J. R. Hunt, Ted Schroeder, W. F. Talbert and R. Falkenburg. The greatest of these, by all accounts, was the first-named, then 25 years of age.

The American ladies were apparently in an even stronger position than the men, with six of the greatest ever seen all straining at the leash to prove their undoubted superiority in all departments. Most of them are famous names to this day; they were the uniquely-talented Miss Louise Brough, Miss Doris Hart, Miss Pauline Betz, Miss Margaret Osborne, Miss Dodo Bundy (a daughter of Miss May Sutton, Wimbledon champion at the turn of the century) and Mrs Pat Todd. Like Alice Marble (and to a lesser degree Sarah Palfrey) these were six of the new young women of tennis – aggressive, dedicated and intent on playing like men. That they should all 'come good' at the same time was little short of miraculous. It was a toss-up which of the six would be the first post-war world singles champion, although most money was on Pauline Betz and Margaret Osborne, who, in fact, met in the Queen's Club final a week before Wimbledon and proved how well matched they were, with Miss Betz running out the winner by a narrow margin.

Despite valiant efforts by the staff, Wimbledon was not quite perfect in time for the re-opening fortnight in the summer of 1946. Materials for rebuilding were in desperately short supply and about 1,100 bomb-damaged seats adjoining the Centre Court were impossible to repair in time and had to be roped off. In a way, this was no bad thing, as a reminder – particularly to visiting Americans, some of whom were making their first visit to Europe – of what Britain and the All-England Club had gone through in the seven years since the last tournament.

In the main, however, the fourteen grass courts (and the nine hard courts) that composed the club were in fairly good shape. The head groundsman, Edwin Fuller, had called in all the casual help he could to supplement his slowly-returning-from-the-services permanent staff, and tried hard to get the best he could out of the war-weary turves with the tired tools and makeshift materials then to hand.

The Centre Court, in particular, had been nursed and renovated for months in an attempt to make it again what it had undoubtedly been in 1939, the fastest court in the world. The previous autumn the ground had been 'chipped' with little forks to prepare it for the descent of nearly a ton of seed. Top dressing with soil and an organic fertiliser had followed, when the growth was strong enough to take this, and some mowing had gradually been introduced, but even the light rollers were kept away from it until the spring. Then mowing in earnest was begun, with added surface dressing of soil mixed with both organic and inorganic fertiliser. Hand weeding, more mowing (gradually getting it down close to ground level) and rolling (longways and crossways with a 35-cwt. roller) completed the process, so that on the day the beautiful turves were again a perfect evenness of firm but fast billard-table-like grass, each blade only one-eighth of an inch in length.

A week before the tournament, half the 14 grass courts had been covered with canvas sheets, the better to make them dry (and fast), with those on the centre and number one courts being hoisted like marquees every night to allow the air to pass through. When the time came, therefore, all was ready on the outer courts for practice during what had become known as 'overseas week', when players unfamiliar with the famous courts of the All-England Club were allowed to have half-an-hour each at a time, between 11 a.m. and 8 p.m., Wednesday to Saturday immediately before the 'fortnight'. As can be imagined, there were more players in 1946 than ever before who had never had sight or smell of Wimbledon, but the new referee somehow contrived to see that everyone had a fair share of the courts.

Play in the tournament itself started then, as now, at 2 p.m. each day, to allow the ground-staff to do any mowing or rolling necessary (usually if strong, acrobatic play had ruffled the turf the previous day) and to mark out the courts for play with whiting (used because it can be erased easily in the event of a mistake. Meanwhile, long queues were forming for the principal courts and matches. The sport-starved British were hungry for action.

Unknown to any of them at the time, the ground staff at Wimbledon were to have more problems from 1946 on than they had ever had before, for the very good reason that post-war tennis was a very different thing from the 'gentlemanly' and 'ladylike' affair it had largely been in its first 75 years. In short, 'professionalism' had now invaded the amateur game, and lawn tennis was now being played (at Wimbledon level, at least) with much more force, speed and power. Rocket services and hard-hitting returns had become the order of the day, and a full quiver of strokes, plus the ability to place a ball on a sixpence any-where in the opposite court, was now less highly regarded among players (although regretted, in its loss, by spectators). The more toes and heels that were dug in, denoting extreme physical endeavour, the more balls that tore into the grass, the tougher life became for Mr Fuller and his staff. But tennis could not stand still any more than any other sport could do. The brave new world was producing thrusting men and women of action and of ambition and this was reflected in the style in which top men and women played the game of their choice.

The betting on the men's singles reached record proportions in the first few days of the 1946 tournament, and with the form unavailable to most of the British punters, a new favourite tended to emerge each day on rumours of this or that sighting in training. The public, having been denied major sport and the thrill of watching stars in the making for more than half a decade were hungry and thirsty for everything short of blood. They broke all attendance records, therefore, in the second week of the championships, and greatly enjoyed themselves.

Jack Kramer was not the obvious favourite he must seem in retrospect, for the good reason that he was a doubles champion and had yet to show his hand in top-class singles (having had his career in the States interrupted by war service). In any event, this was not to be his great year, because he had developed a trouble-some blister on his playing hand which grew fiery as the fortnight proceeded and eventually caused him to be knocked out in the fourth round to one of the few fancied Europeans, 24-year-old Jaroslav Drobny of Czechoslovakia. Pancho Segura, too, of

Ecuador (who had caught many fancies at the London Grass Courts Championship) had gone down to American rival, Tom Brown, in four sets, in the first important Centre Court match of the fortnight.

The other strongly-fancied visitor had been Dinny Pails of Australia. But, like Segura and Kramer, neither Drobny nor Pails paid dividends for their backers. Pails (who had triumphed over Budge Patty) lost in the fifth round to the Indo-China-born French giant, 30-year-old Yvon Petra, while Drobny went out to the two-handed player, G. E. 'Geoff' Brown (another Aussie) in the semi-final. This totally changed situation caused most money to be switched quickly to Tom Brown of California (who had easily k.o.'d Britain's Tony Mottram in straight sets), only for him to go down to the Tilden-like Petra in the other semi-final – making Geoff Brown new favourite. Even that was not to be, because the Australian eventually lost a tremendously hard-fought final to give the voluble, excitable Petra the title after what was, undoubtedly, the most topsy-turvy final ever.

This tournament had offered something totally new in lawn tennis. A fresh spirit was undoubtedly abroad. Never before had there been so many talented players disputing and counter-disputing the Wimbledon title. Wimbledon 1946 was the talk of several continents for weeks afterwards.

Nor was the talk confined to the men's events. Although it had been widely acknowledged that the final of the ladies' singles was certain to be an all-American affair, there had been a fair amount of dispute about which two all-American girls would be the finalists. Disappointingly for those who put their money on relative outsiders, the match results more or less followed the form shown at Queen's Club, at least up to the semi-final stage.

Miss Pauline Betz had no difficulty (to British chagrin) of disposing of our latest young hope, Miss Joy Gannon, for the loss of only one game, while her world-beating compatriots were sorting each other out in the other half of the draw – Miss Brough beating Mrs Todd; Miss Osborne defeating Miss Hart. So it was that although, in the semi-final Miss Brough was able to beat her doubles partner, Miss Osborne, in two strongly disputed sets (while Miss Betz was beating Miss Dodo Bundy 6–2, 6–3), she could only take six games from the all-conquering Miss Betz in a fascinating but predictable Centre Court match that drew a capacity crowd. Louise Brough, the big-hitting, serve-smash-volley expert, played as well as ever but was clearly out-smarted by Pauline Betz's intelligent strategic baseline tactics, based (like Fred Perry's, and Mrs Jean Nicholl-Bostock's) on table tennis. In her six matches up to and including the final (she having had a bye in the first round) the brilliant Miss Betz, one of the truly-great 'greats' of Wimbledon, had lost only 20 games.

It was in 1947 that the bang-bang strong-man style of Big Game tennis, introduced to Wimbledon in 1946, really came into its own, with the high priest himself, the immensely fit Big Jack Kramer, making his unforgettable mark on Wimbledon, while endearing himself to the public by his straight-shooting life-style and complete lack of guile or gamesmanship.

The tall, tough, rugged, lean Kramer was in every respect a phenomenal tennis player, possessing as he did a powerful, big-hitting, all-court game, with few weaknesses in it anywhere. He was also a fine sportsman and the sort of personality to whom the Wimbledon crowds quickly warm. He was so far ahead of his time in the 'forties that he changed the course of championship lawn tennis in a way that is still reverberating today.

Kramer had used the serve-and-volley tactics from his earliest tennis days, at the start of the war, that were to change the long-established balance between net and baseline play, but they were now being seen in circumstances which were to influence every strong young player in the game. He had learned his rocket service, ball control and stroke production from Ellsworth Vines, while still in his teens, and, through concentrated coaching, had built up also a Tilden-style game (but with more emphasis on consistent attacking from the net), employing the Eastern grip that had made him, as a youngster, one of the finest match players in the business. Above all things, he possessed the iron will of the dependable winner. Kramer's war interlude, in the Marines, had been short enough not to take the edge off his game, although it had meant that he played no tennis whatsoever in the months of his service in 1944 and 1945.

The modern game of lawn tennis, as personified more in the great Australians of recent years than in the great Americans, is widely acknowledged to stem from the volleying game of Jack Kramer, based on sheer domination of the net in a way it had never been dominated before, without subtlety – every service (first or second) and every service return, being resolutely followed by an advance to the net, there to volley a winner first time if humanly possible, in the belief that the longer he was at the net the more chance his opponent had of making a successful passing stroke. It was the bang-bang of the Big Game and a new concept. 'I either win fast or I lose fast' was how Kramer put it.

As stated, Jack Kramer was chiefly different from the big hitters who had gone before him, in seventy years of world championships on grass at Wimbledon (including Vines, Budge and Tilden), and from the fast-accurate volleyers (like Perry, Cochet and the big-serving-plus-net-playing Vines) in that he persistently went to the net on virtually every point, where the most aggressive of his predecessors had restricted their following-through volleys to opportunist advances. But he was a traditionalist to the point that he used the Eastern grip for the forehand drive (with the palm of the hand parallel with the racket face and flat against the back of the handle) in the manner of Tilden, Vines, Budge, Petra and many others. This was, in truth, becoming the most popular of the three or four grips then in vogue. The English one, favoured by Crawford, von Cramm, Austin, (and Suzanne Lenglen), was fading. So was the Continental one of Perry, Cochet, Lacost, etc.

Kramer served in a way only equalled then by Drobny. The throwing up of the ball and the swinging of the racket were performed in one simple movement, in perfect rhythm and timing, known by heart, there being no need to look at the ball. And he followed through by playing many of his power-packed volleys against the fast service-returns of opponents standing even inside the baseline. What he introduced that was novel was smash-and-grab attacking, with speed allied to athleticism, allowing full advantage to be taken of vicious serving and fearful volleying. With Jack Kramer, lawn tennis grew up, becoming in him both professional (in the true sense of the relentless pursuit of perfection) and spectacular.

By 1947, Kramer was probably at the height of his undoubted powers. That summer, fit as the proverbial fiddle, he raided the All-England Club and took away the singles trophies as if they had been locked up in a paper bag. In a sequence of matches as devastating as it was dazzling, he defeated W. J. Moss, 6–0, 6–1, 6–0; C. Cucelli, 6–0, 6–2, 6–0; T. Johansson, 7–5, 6–2, 6–3;

Geoff Brown, 6–0, 6–1, 6–3; Dinny Pails, 6–1, 3–6, 6–1, 6–0, and Tom Brown, 6–1, 6–3, 6–2. Nothing quite like it had been seen before at Wimbledon. The crowds that had turned out in record numbers to see the great new lawn tennis 'king' saw instead a display of almost machine-like domination that eventually began to pall and to bore in its greatness. It was, in any event, Wimbledon's first and last opportunity to see 'Jake' (as he was then called) Kramer at his brilliant best.

Dedicated 'professional' that he had undoubtedly been since he had first become schoolboy champion of the U.S.A. in 1936, at the age of 15, the straight-shooting Californian had never made any mystery of his intentions – viz that he would turn 'pro' whenever an attractive offer was made to him. Not many weeks after the 1947 Wimbledon fortnight, at which he had so effortlessly shown his true greatness, Kramer was offered a record fee of $70,000 to do so and signed the necessary documents in November, 1947, taking his Big Game to the lucrative 'bowls' of the big-money tennis circus.

In the amateur game, Kramer (who had been undefeated in any tournament for 12 months) had been so far ahead of the opposition that his continuing presence might have resulted in a loss of competitive interest, in the men's singles at least; and in the professional ranks, too, he had no superiors and precious few peers. Over a period of years, he convincingly beat Riggs, Gonzalez, Sedgman and others; he also became an able and trusted professional tennis administrator. Today, he is regarded as probably the shrewdest tennis commentator-assessor ever. His Big Game was a turning point in tennis. In his hands, it was Great as well as Big. In the hands of some of his successors, it has tended, perhaps, to lead too much to a tiresome sequence of short points, with far too little stroke play.

Kramer's loss to amateur tournaments did not mean that the U.S. was in decline in this field. In fact, in the immediately post-Kramer era, America began to gain a fresh marked ascendency through the advent of a sequence of talented not to say brilliant, players. These were led by Frank Parker, Gardnar Mulloy, Bill Talbert, Robert Falkenburg, Budge Patty and Victor Seixas, with even younger aspirants of great promise already around, in Pancho Gonzales, William Larned and Herbert Flam. Australia, by comparison, was going through a pretty thin time of it (especially with Dinny Pails, too, having turned 'pro', and John Bromwich due to retire in 1948) and Europe was running a poor third.

Britain most of all, had struck its bleakest point in the men's competitions for many years, with no Englishman having been able to reach the last 16 at Wimbledon, 1947, for the first time in living memory.

Nor were our post-war women doing much better. Although Mrs Jean Bostock (née Nicholls) had made the last eight, it was a solo performance of no great merit and she was convincingly beaten by Miss Doris Hart.

Young Americans were about to win the next four men's singles titles at Wimbledon – 1948–49–50–51 – while American girls would win these and every other Wimbledon singles' title well up to the end of the 'fifties, with the Big Game on everybody's lips as *the* style for players of both sexes – but, alas, without the Kramer-style Big Game ever being fully understood or fully reproduced by anyone after the master had moved on.

Chapter Nine / Two-handed to Victory

Robert Falkenburg was taller than Kramer (with whom he had had a successful doubles partnership) and played a somewhat-similar Big Game, featuring a cannonball service of comparable speed and power. But he was judged by Wimbledon not to be the sportsman his compatriot had always been found to be. Where Jack Kramer could do no wrong, in the eyes of the Church Road crowds, Bob Falkenburg could do little right.

In 1948, Kramer having turned 'pro' and made the singles event more open than it had been for some time, the seeded men players at Wimbledon were Parker, Bromwich, Mulloy, Tom Brown, Drobny, Patty, Falkenburg and Sturgess, in that order, making a Parker-Bromwich final the one pointed to by the betting. In the event, Falkenburg's win was therefore as unexpected as it was to prove unwelcome.

Unseeded Lennart Bergalin of Sweden knocked out the number one seed in the fourth round, after Italy's unseeded champion, G. Cucelli, had put out the number five seed, Jaroslav Drobny, in five sets, and Cucelli was in turn defeated by Britain's Tony Mottram in a tremendously exciting match. Meanwhile, the 23-year-old Falkenburg, seeded seven, but rather weak on stamina, had been coming in for criticism and barracking on his way to the final, because of his displays of temper and his gamesmanship, which included long rests between points. Indeed, in the semi-final against his fellow-American Gardnar Mulloy (who had k.o.'d Mottram in the quarter finals) he toppled over many times in the course of lunging for wide balls, thereafter to lie on the grass for longish periods, to the annoyance of the crowd and his opponent.

97

The veteran John Bromwich of Australia (a great favourite with the Wimbledon crowds) had meanwhile won through to the final in the other half of the draw. He was 30, or eight years older than Falkenburg. But the Wimbledon crowds are notorious for supporting older men against young talent, and Falkenburg was already out of favour.

There was therefore some resentment in the crowd when, in the final, Falkenburg somewhat ostentatiously threw away the second set, 0–6, against Bromwich in a Borotra-like tactic (lacking, alas, the Borotra voluble charm) to pace himself, and to allow his tired body to recover from over-exhaustion brought about by a hard-fought first set (which had gone to 7–5) against an opponent who played a totally different and unorthodox baseline game, based on an always-accurate return of serve plus an unmatched quiver of bang-on passing shots.

Not only did Falkenburg throw away the second. Having won the third by 6–2, and again showing signs of fatigue, he also chose to throw away the fourth without much fight with the idea of conserving all his power for the final set. But neither he nor Bromwich rose to the occasion. The final set was dull, almost to boredom, with the barracking of the crowd the only real relief every time that Falkenburg threatened to stall or fox for any reason. The two-handed Bromwich, who could have won the championship without too much trouble, was actually poised at 5–3 and 40–15 at one point. But he injudiciously threw it all away by the lack of speed in all his shots while playing for safety, and handed the American the title on a plate at 7–5.

The Press attacked Falkenburg in the days that followed the fortnight, accusing him of foxing unnecessarily, and even of cheating. The mighty Brig. J. G. Smythe, of the *Sunday Times,* went so far as to say that he would be failing in his duty to lawn tennis if he did not condemn roundly Falkenburg's stalling tactics. The American replied that he found the Wimbledon crowd partisan and unsporting. He also described the Church Road officials as the most biased and prejudiced he had ever encountered. In his favour, it must be said that he obviously lacked the stamina to play at full speed for five long sets, and he sensibly paced himself with this in mind.

In the ladies' singles of 1948, Britain managed two players in the last eight, Mrs Jean Bostock and Miss Jean Quertier. But the Americans were as dominant as ever, with Miss Brough only just beating Miss Hart in the final for the second year running.

Fresh young players were now bringing with them their own varied styles. In addition to Bromwich, who had followed Vivian McGrath in the new involved two-handed style of play (except that it was forehand in Bromwich's case, where it had been backhand in McGrath's) two new two-handed players had made their debut at Wimbledon in the strong shapes of Francesco 'Pancho' Segura of Ecuador and Geoff Brown of Australia. Segura was different from his predecessors in that he stroked on both wings with two hands; and Brown used both hands solely for drives and volleys to the forehand.

At the 63rd Wimbledon Championship meeting in 1949, the demand for tickets was greater than the All-England Club had ever experienced. The probable reason was that every top amateur in the world was due to play, with only a couple of exceptions. Contrarily, Bob Falkenburg had also become an attraction. He had become the man to hate, and when he found himself opposed once again to John Bromwich, but in the quarter-finals this time, the crowd assumed erroneously that they would be seeing a 'grudge' match. In fact, the tennis this time was good and so was the sportsmanship. After Falkenburg had won the first two tough sets, he was obviously exhausted and proceeded to lose the next three while putting up as strong a fight as he had ever done. Bromwich well deserved his 'revenge', and this time Falkenburg generously acknowledged the fact.

In the fourth round, the new two-handed Australian, little Geoff Brown, had surprised everyone by knocking out Richard 'Pancho' Gonzales, the new American champion, in four sets, and Brown's double-handed forehand drives had played a notable part in the victory.

The ultimate winner in 1949 (Brown and Bromwich both having gone down to Drobny) was a pipe-smoking Californian, 'Lucky' Ted Schroeder (who had been one of Jack Kramer's favourite partners), seeded number two to Gonzales but about eight years older than Pancho. Oddly, although Schroeder had been a notable Davis Cup success for very many years, this had been his very first Wimbledon appearance. True to form, he took five long sets (during which he joked, grimaced and rolled around) to overcome Drobny, but in the process he gave the crowd the best value for their money for years, in entertainment as well as in sport. It was both his debut and his swansong at Church Road, but during the sporting and cheerful appearances that he made during the fortnight, the lionhearted 28-year-old Frederick Rudolf ('Ted' for short) Schroeder became a tremendous favourite with the record crowds who attended that 1949 meeting.

In other matches, America again dominated the ladies' singles, although Britain put up the best show for years by getting four players into the last eight – Mrs Walker-Smith, Mrs Blair, Mrs Hilton and Mrs Dawson-Scott. The final, between Miss Brough and Mrs du Pont, lasted a full two hours, with the third and final set taking nearly an hour, and hardly a point splitting them until Mrs Brough succeeded at 8–8 in exhausting her compatriot and finishing her off at 10–8.

By contrast with 1949, when nearly everyone of note in world tennis playing at Wimbledon, 1950 saw quite a few absentees and a confused pattern in the men's seeding. Pancho Gonzales, who had never shown his best form at Wimbledon, had turned professional (after only two years at the top) at 21 years of age, having beaten Ted Schroeder for his second American championship a few months before and having been freely talked about as the world's leading amateur; Ted Schroeder had failed to show up to defend his title; top Australian, Frank Sedgman, seeded one, was considered unfit; and there were notable missing persons in the lists.

A fresh number one seed from the U.S. was making his first appearance at Wimbledon – at the astonishing age of 32. He was Billy Talbert, a doctor, who had been number three in America to Gonzales and Schroeder for some time, while mainly specialising in doubles. No British player made the last 16, which was almost a worst-ever performance. Drobny was there, as was the ageing John Bromwich. Both were out of it by the semi-final stage. All in all, it was an unexciting tournament, but a new big name established itself in Budge Patty, the eventual winner, who had k.o.'d Talbert along the line and who delighted an enthusiastic following with his artistic stroke production.

Patty, another Californian, who had lived in France a lot, was himself 26 by now. He had been junior U.S. champion as long ago as 1941. Like every other leading player with the strength and ambition to be number one, he was now rushing the net at every opportunity, in the Kramer Big Game fashion; but he was naturally an all-court player of some brilliance, of whom much more would be heard at Wimbledon in the years to come.

In the women's events in 1950, the same depressing (for Britain) story continued, as the American ladies relentlessly steam-rollered the rest. Miss Doris Hart had fully recovered from the eye injury that had prevented her appearance in 1949, and was present with her brilliant Wightman Cup colleagues. Britain had only one seed, Mrs C. Harrison, who until the week before had been Betty Hilton. As she was on her honeymoon during the Wimbledon fortnight not too much was expected of her . . . nor offered. In the end, it was again Miss Louise Brough who took the title, having convincingly beaten Miss Hart in the semi-final and the fading Mrs du Pont in the final. This was Miss Brough's third Wimbledon title in a row (and, additionally, she had a hat-trick of events won at Church Road by the end of the fort-night), which equalled the record of Mrs Helen Wills-Moody.

Although Miss Doris Hart was to win Wimbledon as she had so long deserved to do, in an immaculate display of tennis, by 6–1, 6–0 against Miss Shirley Fry in 1951 (after the equally-talented Mrs du Pont had gone out in three sets to the new American youngster, the ambidexterous Miss Beverley Baker) the reigns of the famous American 'queens of the courts' of the 'fifties was in decline, and new names were springing to every-one's lips around the courts at Church Road. Notable among them was that of Miss Althea Gibson – and the more so because she was a *coloured* American. This was something new, indeed.

On the men's side, too, there was lots of new young talent – notably Herbert Flam, Richard Savitt and Hamilton Richardson (all of America), the last named being only 17 years of age. There were no British players in the ten seeds for the Wimble-don men's singles, so the many patriots among the spectators prepared to favour Frank Sedgman and Ken McGregor ('king of the doubles'), both of Australia, and Eric Sturgess of South Africa. But America was again dominant, with five fine seeds in Mulloy, Flam, Larsen, Savitt and Patty, and then there was the ever-present Jaroslav Drobny (now living in Egypt) to be con-sidered. Interestingly, while Sedgman was again number one seed, Drobny was elevated to number two.

In the betting, Drobny – partly based on sentiment for an ageing warhorse who had given marvellous entertainment without ever being top dog, and partly because he had had an excellent season – was favourite for a time, and much was the surprise when Tony Mottram rose to the occasion and knocked out the Egyptian-Czech in an exciting five-setter (only to be put out himself by the Swedish stylist, L. Bergelin). Another unseeded player, the teenaged Hamilton Richardson, added to the upsets of 1951 by k.o.'ing the holder, Budge Patty, in the second round, again in five sets; and the new young generation then took top blood when Sedgman went out to Herbert Flam. The semi-final was Flam v. Savitt and Sturgess v. McGregor ... and, in a disappointing final, Ken McGregor (against all expectations) went down to the tall, powerful Dick Savitt (who had won the Australian championship a few months before, and had a formidable range of ground strokes but was otherwise a less-than-glamorous figure to the crowds).

The Wimbledon fortnight of 1952 was recognised as the seventy-fifth birthday of the All-England Club's tennis adventures, so it was something of an occasion in the town. The courts had been prettied-up and more spectator accommodation had been provided, although the 30,000 places available could probably have been sold twice over, having to be balloted for, as had been the case for a considerable time. The main change behind the scenes was that Colonel W. T. Legg had taken over as championship referee from Captain A. K. Trower, who had died in harness.

Again the news from abroad was of a great new young American girl (and this time it was 100 per cent the truth) who was sweeping all before her. The name was Maureen Connolly.

'Little Mo' Connolly, coached by the legendary Eleanor 'Teach' Tennant, who had taught Alice Marble, was quickly to become the greatest lady power player ever to grace Wimbledon and was to die tragically of cancer, at the age of only 34, just before the first open Wimbledon in 1968.

'Little Mo' had been given her nickname (because of her tough, hard-hitting play and her extensive armoury of strokes) after the world's most powerful battleship of the time, the U.S.S. Missouri, which was known as 'Big Mo'. She had astonishingly captured the U.S. singles' championship in 1951, when sweet

16, and was now to triumph at Wimbledon (where she would never lose a singles' match or a singles' set on the Centre Court) in 1952, 1953, and 1954, aged only 17, 18 and 19, after which she was to be prevented from beating Helen Wills-Moody's run of Wimbledon championships by a ghastly riding accident in 1954, which was to injure a leg badly and stop her playing any more competitive lawn tennis.

But back in 1952, her first year of triumph in England, the crowds, agog to see her play, were not disappointed. Extraordinarily, she seemed to be as strong on the backhand as with her unmatchably-powerful forehand, either flat or with a slight controlling roll, and all her strokes seemed steadily sustained in speed and power, no matter how long a match lasted. In the final of 1952, she wore down the talented Louise Brough with hard-hitting drives against which the more experienced American could find no answer, the number one seed, Miss Hart, having gone out earlier to her compatriot Mrs Todd.

In the men's singles, despite the perennial young challenge, the older player prevailed, with the first two seeds, Sedgman and Drobny, meeting in the final. The crowd's loyalties were split down the middle on this occasion, with the Australian having to share the waves of sentimental affection with the Czech. Drobny was in top form on the Centre Court, and won the first set in sterling fashion. But he later wilted and faded, when Sedgman turned to all-out attack, and was once more cheated of the championship title he had so long desired.

It was a turning-point in another way, however. Dapper Frank Sedgman had broken the incredible run of American successes and was taking the singles title to Australia for the first time since 1933. This was a remarkable performance by the 25-year-old super-fit, power-volleying Australian, and it is worth recording that he had not dropped a set in the last three rounds against Mervyn Rose, Eric Sturgess and Jaroslav Drobny. Australian fans, in an attempt to keep their idol an amateur, had made a gift of over £5,000 to Sedgman's bride at their marriage, but he nevertheless turned professional, as most world champions had done before him, not long after Wimbledon.

The ladies' singles final in the following year, 1953, when 'Little Mo' Connolly beat Doris Hart 8–6, 7–5, was undoubtedly one of the finest women's matches ever played, and is talked about to this day by those who were present. And when Maureen beat Miss Brough (four times a Wimbledon winner) for the second time in three years in the 1954 final, conceding only one more game than in 1952, her bubbling personality was trumpeted to echo in the bowl of the Centre Court for all time.

The rest of the 'fifties in women's tennis were less entertaining for her absence through retirement. The old-stagers continued for a time, with Louise Brough gaining another singles win on the Centre Court in 1955; and then Althea Gibson, of the coffee-coloured skin and the Big Game of serve-and-volley, triumphed, as she deserved to do, at Wimbledon in 1957 and 1958, before turning professional and eventually switching successfully to golf, like others before.

Another Australian, of whom much would be heard into the 'seventies, made his top-line debut in 1953 when he carried off the French championship, as well as his own national title. He was Kenny Rosewall. But it was an American, slender, dark and handsome 30-year-old, Big-Game-playing Vic Seixas (a temperamental, wayward Adonis from Philadelphia who charmed women spectators and upset men, as he stormed his way through his matches) who took the Wimbledon title that year; he also went into the history books with a run, starting in 1953, as the first man to win the mixed doubles four times in a row – the first three with Doris Hart and the last time (in 1956) with Shirley Fry. He then retired at the mature age (for tennis) of 34 and became a banker.

To the delight of his many long-faithful fans, bespectacled Jaroslav Drobny (twice runner-up) at last made it third time lucky, in 1954, when, in what was probably the most emotion-packed final of all time, he defeated Ken Rosewall to take the men's singles title (for which he had been competing since 1939 and in which he had been seeded no less than eight times). Now a naturalised Englishman, Drobny still receives the acclaim of the Wimbledon crowds when he turns up to watch during the championships, or to play in the veterans' matches. He was, incidentally, the first left-hander to win at Wimbledon for forty years – the last having been also the first (the great Jack Crawford). Nor would there be another until the all-left-handed final of 1960, when Neale Fraser defeated the young Rod Laver.

America fought back to the top in 1955 in the shape of 25-

year-old Cincinnati-born Tony Trabert. Taller than his friend Seixas, and more solidly built, he used the heavy artillery of serve, smash and volley in a disconcertingly smooth-stroking manner to pummel his opponents into beaten pulp. He had won the U.S. singles in 1953 and 1955, without conceding a set, and he repeated this triumph at Wimbledon. Not surprisingly, Trabert turned professional a few weeks after his success at Church Road.

In Trabert's absence, a great new personality came to the top at Wimbledon – fair-haired, thick-set Aussie, Lew Hoad. He had grown up as a 'twin' of Ken Rosewall (in neighbouring Sydney suburbs) and they had played together or in opposition since their schooldays, before being taken in hand by the great coach, Harry Hopman, as teenagers. Together they had won the Wimbledon doubles when only 18, and then Lew Hoad, at 21 and again at 22 years of age, had used his tremendous service and deceptive half-volley to win the singles twice in succession. The years were in 1956 and 1957, and the wins first by 6–2, 4–6, 7–5, 6–4, in a marvellous fluctuating final four-set match against Rosewall, and then in a one-sided final against fellow-Aussie, Ashley Cooper in 50 minutes, at 6–2, 6–1, 6–2. Hoad then accepted a tempting offer to turn professional, and so joined his pal Rosewall, who had become a pro in 1956 after winning the U.S. singles. His nonchalant manner and apparently easy style hid the fact that he was one of the most powerful power-players of all time. Nor was he lacking in a range of strokes. Indeed, it was the shrewd opinion of Sir Norman Brookes that, in this respect, Hoad was second only to Tilden in the history of tennis.

Ashley Cooper, another Harry Hopman discovery, kept the Australian flag flying at Wimbledon the following year when, at 21, he took the 1958 singles title, but the departure of Rosewall and Hoad for the Kramer circus before they had even reached their peak (to be followed soon after by Ashley Cooper) weakened Australian tennis at a time when Australia looked like going on and on as the most invincible country in the world, equally on lawns and hardcourts.

Throughout the 'fifties one male star had brightly winked and blinked in the sky without ever, regrettably, blazing to success at Wimbledon. This was the star of Nicola Pietrangeli, who was probably the finest hardcourt player in the world by 1958–59, but who never quite made it on grass. The 26-year-old Tunisian-born Italian was to appear 16 times at Wimbledon, during his otherwise-meteoric career, without ever getting beyond the quarter-finals (in 1954) and the semi-finals (in 1960). It was the greatest of pities, because Wimbledon was by now in desperate need of finalists of Pietrangeli's calibre.

Chapter Ten / The Years of Decline

Towards the end of the 'fifties and for almost a decade thereafter Wimbledon suffered a decline in prestige that was extremely hurtful to all connected with it, and particularly to the officials who had fought so hard over the years to ensure that the famous ground of the All-England Lawn Tennis and Croquet Club should hold its position as the site of the greatest tennis tournament in the world. The fault did not in fact lie with the officials, or with the Wimbledon courts, or with local administration of the game. It had been brought about, inevitably and inexorably, by the ever-quicker drain of top players to the professional ranks that had been building up over twenty years or so. It was adding up, more and more, to the fact that the professional circus was offering the public displays by all the best players of the period, while Wimbledon was often having to make do with tired-looking second-best players, while looking and hoping for the magic of new young talent. It is difficult to recall just how bitterly the honest and amiable Jack Kramer was regarded in those days for his enterprise and good business sense. 'Pirate' was the pseudonym most often applied to him. It is easy, on the other hand, to see the terror he was causing in the hearts of the joint committee running Wimbledon. It was as plain to them that the magic that had built Church Road was ebbing away year after year. Winning Wimbledon was becoming a lever which the best amateurs were able to use to increase the amounts of money being offered to them to turn professional (and so be lost to Wimbledon). It was the most vicious spiral, and the bottom of it was too depressing to contemplate.

The truth of the matter was based on a precept as old as the

hills of Worple Road. Grey personalities make grey entertainment. In sport (as in showbusiness) the tightrope between success
and failure is precarious; not only were bright personalities
needed to fill Wimbledon; the fact was, Wimbledon was also
competing with other sports and other stadia for public support,
and if Kramer's circus went on creaming off every young prospect, there would be little in prospect for Wimbledon other than
decline and fall.

So it was that the grumbles and sweats and head-scratchings
began in the back rooms of Wimbledon in 1959 that were to
find sensible fulfilment in 1968 with open tennis. Nine years
may seem a long time to bring this about, but in fact it is fairly
quick for so dyed-in-the-establishment-wool an organisation as
the All-England Club; and the fact remains that it *did* win
through by looking after its own interests and so maintained
Wimbledon to this day as the greatest lawn tennis club in the
world.

Anyway, in 1959, the men's singles title was wide open once
more with Cooper also having gone over the the pro's. In the
event, the star of the tournament turned out to be the first seed,
Peruvian Alex Olmedo, who had had his tennis education in the
States (like Mexican world champ, Pancho Gonzales, before
him), and it was then to be his turn, of course, to join the
Kramer circus after beating the raw, unseeded Rod Laver, in the
Wimbledon singles final, by 6–4, 6–3, 6–4.

1960, as already recounted, featured the final of the left-
handers, when Neale Fraser (who had 'blown up' in the final
against Ashley Cooper two years before) somehow survived an
even more exhausting cliff-hanger against Rod Laver. It was a
final in which Frazer took chance after chance to defeat the
tough red-haired Queenslander, whose own great day was coming
very soon, and who was having his second toughening in succession on the Centre Court, at 21, by 6–4, 3–6, 9–7, and 7–5.

Meanwhile, in 1959, women's tennis had had a splendid
boost with the arrival on the scene of the lovely and talented
Brazilian, Maria Bueno – perhaps the most delightful mover ever
to be seen on the Centre Court. So glamorous a figure was Maria
that the first of her three Wimbledon successes was commemorated
by the issue of a special postage stamp in Brazil.

Born the daughter of a doctor at Sao Paulo on the 11th of

October, 1939, Maria was blessed with many gifts with the notable exception of consistently good health. The result was that after winning Wimbledon brilliantly in 1959, and repeating the performance in 1960, with an all-court display and a quiver of strokes and that had the crowds sighing with delight, she abdicated abruptly through ill-health and was out of tennis until 1963. Then she quickly built up star quality again to complete the hat-trick of Wimbledon victories in 1964, and was runner-up to Margaret Smith in 1965.

1961, however, was Britain's year, as far as the ladies were concerned. It would be ungracious, perhaps, to say that Angela Mortimer took the singles title because Miss Bueno did not defend it, although there is undoubtedly some truth in this. A painstaking player, Angela had commuted from Devon over the years to win her way through the Wimbledon Juniors, the British Covered Courts, the British Hard Courts, the Wimbledon Doubles and other 'almost there' events, and had actually beaten Doris Hart and Shirley Fry consecutively, when each was ranked world's number one, in the Wightman Cup singles. Now she had her moment of glory when she defeated Christine Truman in a final which had the schoolgirls present twittering and squeaking with delight. An able tactician, Angela would go on to captain the Wightman Cup team before retiring in 1971 to have a baby as Mrs John Barrett. Angela did not defend her title in 1962, when Mrs J. R. Susman (née K. Hantze) defeated Mrs V. Sukova, 6–4, 6–4, in an extremely unmemorable final.

Wimbledon was in obvious decline. Although tickets were still selling well, people were going along more to be seen (and to talk about it afterwards) than from any sense of having hitched their wagons to unreachable stars. Another danger sign was that personalities were so thin on the ground, around the many courts in use during the fortnight, that the crowds tended to be bored and restive where they had once been quiet and reverent.

Officials in the general office at Church Road noticed it in an increasing volume of complaints stemming from disappointment and irritation; umpires were deeply aware of the decline as they grouped restlessly in front of their retiring room and assessed the all-too-familiar scene; commissionaires observed it in the faces of the still-queuing standing room area at the Centre Court; players reflected upon it, as they looked out unhappily from their glass-fronted enclosure high above the arenas, where the glum faces could be seen, of fans reluctantly assembled to do some sort of homage to a fading veteran or to an alleged 'exciting' newcomer, boosted before his time and beyond his powers.

Astonishingly, young people still slept on the pavements overnight (some for as long as 24 hours) in a manner otherwise reserved for the Proms, and the Beatles, seeking some remembered or hoped for thrill unique to Wimbledon. In 1961 and 1962, praise be, they had their moments of fulfilled satisfaction if they were able to see the men's final (although the ladies were a below-par lot). Those were the only occasions in the sixties (until open Wimbledon came along at the end of the decade) that perhaps the greatest male player of all time, in the Big Game pattern, could be seen at Church Road – the incomparable Rod Laver.

What is to be said about Laver that has not been declared already? The new message here perhaps is that because of the ridiculous pro-amateur conflicts that were wrecking the tennis world, the modern champion of champions was, perhaps, never really seen at his peak on the lawns of the world mecca of lawn tennis. The whipcord wrist and forehand, which he carefully nurtured to an unmatched strength in a player of his size, were at their strongest in the *mid*-sixties, when he was absent from Wimbledon altogether.

In the first of the two years when Laver completely dominated Wimbledon in the early 'sixties, and added some sparkle to the lean years at Church Road, he defeated the sturdy American, Chuck McKinley, in 57 minutes by 6–3, 6–1, 6–4. And in the following year, 1962, the small wiry left-handed figure in the soft sun-hat played his fantastic Big Game, with its almost-unplayable service, to k.o. his over-awed compatriot, Marty Mulligan, for the loss of only five games, in a scoreline, unusual for the Centre Court, that read 6–2, 6–2, 6–1.

Then, while Laver was earning sums of money previously unthought of around the professional circuits of the tennis world, the Wimbledon title was again slipping into unfashionable hands. In 'the master's' absence in 1963, the short, thick-set Chuck McKinley, thumped a forehand way, by 9–7, 6–1, 6–4, to uninspiring victory over the tall, fair-haired Australian, Fred Stolle – a dedicated but by no means fluid stroke-player. It was

America's first singles win at Wimbledon since her adopted son, Alex Olmedo, had pulled it off in 1959.

Stolle (a great doubles player) then in his mid-twenties, had the record of being the runner-up in singles in more top tournaments than anyone else in the period, and he now went on to establish the extraordinary sequence of three Wimbledon singles finals in a row without one win. In 1964 and 1965 his opponent and victor was the same man, Roy Emerson, and the score-lines read respectively, 6–4, 12–10, 4–6, 6–3 ... and 6–2, 6–4, 6–4. Emerson, like Laver a Queenslander, was Australian champion a record number of times, and was a fine player with a fantastic service, but he never quite made it in the affections of the Wimbledon crowds.

Europe had been having a thin time in top names for some years, but in the mid-sixties a beautiful touch-player came to the fore in the elegant shape of Spaniard Manuel Santana. Like Pietrangeli before him, Santana was better on hard courts than on grass, but in 1966 he succeeded in beating Dennis Ralston of America, 6–4, 11–9, 6–4, to become Wimbledon champion. It should have been the ultimate year of triumph for the superior-playing Roy Emerson, favoured by the bookies and the seeding to become the first man since Fred Perry to win the world's greatest title three times running. Alas, in an early round he injured his ankle in a fall, when playing against Owen Davidson, and lost his chance.

In 1967, the last year of the doldrums for supporters of the men's game at Wimbledon, Australia again showed that she had reserves of talented young players when 23-year-old John Newcombe, of Sydney, became the greatest amateur in the world. Rated only number three in the Antipodes, the powerful, good-looking Newcombe played the Big Game of his life to knock out 28-year-old Wilhelm Bungert of West Germany, in a disappointing and very short final, by 6–3, 6–1, 6–1. Bungert failed completely to rise to the occasion, although, in becoming the first German to reach the Wimbledon final in twenty years, he had succeeded in beating Bobby Wilson, Thomaz Koch and Roger Taylor along the way, each in five sets.

Meanwhile, in the ladies' singles, the other great name of the 'sixties was being heard loudly at last at Wimbledon. In 1963, 20-year-old Margaret Smith, from Albery, N.S.W. (who had been playing at Wimbledon since 1961, and, even as a teenager, had never been seeded lower than two) convincingly overcame Billie-Jean Moffitt – who had beaten her in the first round the year before – by 6–3 and 6–4. But in 1964, the young Australian had to bow to returning 'queen' Maria Bueno, when the Brazilian tigress, happily restored to health, taught her a lesson in fluid and elegant play to become third-time Wimbledon singles champion by 6–4, 7–9, 6–3.

Revenge being sweet, and the powerful Margaret Smith having age on her side, the scoreline in the 1965 final read 6–4, 7–5, in favour of the Australian over the all-court-playing Brazilian. Miss Bueno, the school teacher turned queen of the courts, was fading, alas, and in 1966 she said farewell to Wimbledon, again as runner-up, when the other great lady of the 'sixties and early 'seventies, America's Billie-Jean King (née Moffitt), beat her but did not disgrace her by 6–3, 3–6, 6–4.

The emergence of Billie-Jean Moffitt-King at this time to become the first lady since Doris Hart to win all three Wimbledon titles and the first since Maureen Connolly to be Wimbledon singles champion thrice in a row (in 1966, when she defeated Miss Bueno; in 1967 when Ann Jones was her victim; and in 1968 when it was Judy Tegart's turn) is one of the great stories of modern lawn tennis. Born at Los Angeles in November, 1943, she was no great shakes as a junior, but by talking herself into greatness and working hard at her game she astonished everyone by becoming at least the equal of the other two taller queens of the decade, Miss Bueno and Margaret Smith-Court. A tiny, bespectacled figure, Billie-Jean raised American prestige on the courts at a time when it was sagging badly, and, with her excellent ground-strokes and her Big Game of serve-and-volley, she became a great favourite on the Centre Court – especially as she tongue-lashed herself through every crisis, the most reluctant loser Church Road had ever seen.

Chapter Eleven / Open and Honest

The man who had been responsible since the First World War for keeping the world's most famous court in perfection each year, head groundsman Edwin Fuller, had died in harness in 1966, and there were changes made in the turves themselves, as well as in the administration, before Wimbledon went Open in 1968. Fuller was succeeded by Bob Twynam, as valet to the 10,800 square yards of precious grass, and with the 'new broom' came some new ideas. Not that Twynam was a young man. At 55, he had been on the Wimbledon ground staff for 41 years before becoming head groundsman, having started as a ball boy for the 1925 championship. The principal change he introduced when he settled in was to introduce a slightly coarser and closer-knit form of grass-seed, producing a darker-green shade of turf. His aim was to make the lush grass hard enough to stand up to the ever-rougher treatment given to the surface by the exigencies of big men playing the Big Game more and more.

It was in the winter of 1967–68, after many years of attempts in international committee meetings that had gone off half-cock, that Britain made the overdue but nevertheless welcome decision to go it alone in lawn tennis by staging open tournaments in which professionals and amateurs would play side by side. Politically, this was the most astonishing event in the 90-odd years' history of lawn tennis. It represented a rout of the reactionary diehards who had so long held up progress at the International Lawn Tennis Federation, and it was a vindication of Britain's lawn tennis administrators who had often been accused of being resisters of change.

As had always been the case over the years, the trump card

held by British officials was Wimbledon. It was rightly calculated that if the world's greatest championship meeting went open, the others would have to follow suit or go into decline.

The All-England Club and its affiliated officials had been urgently seeking ways for some time to open Wimbledon to the 'pros'. A brilliant and secret plan had been laid early in 1967 to put the first nail in the coffin of tennis 'shamateurism'. Whereas, except for the hard-courts which are open to members throughout the year, the courts in Church Road were normally closed down immediately after the championship fortnight (except for a minor junior event or occasional Davis Cup matches) so that the brown patches in the grass could be attended to, and other wear-and-tear repairs carried out, in August, 1967, the sacred turves were turned over to the 'enemy', for an all-professional tournament. It was the first time in 10 years or more that some of the 'pros' had been able to step on the turf at Wimbledon, and their resultant pleasure was as great as that of the large crowd of spectators who supported the event.

As a result of this 'misdemeanor' and of rumours that surrounded it, the British Lawn Tennis Association was being threatened with expulsion from the International Lawn Tennis Federation and exclusion from the Davis Cup. But the wrath of the international conservatives seemed a bit silly when measured against the fact that the top amateurs were melting away to the enemy, anyway and that, also in December, 1967, Tony Roche and John Newcombe (the top Australians) plus Britain's Roger Taylor, and other international stars, had banded together to form a professional group calling themselves The Handsome Eight.

The astute All-England-plus-L.T.A. committee were meanwhile working semi-secretly towards opening up the 1968 Wimbledon tournament, so that there would be no distinctions between professionals and amateurs, and so that the faithful customers would be given *all* the big names for the first time for very many years. Britain's hoisting of the Jolly Roger was no sudden decision. The All-England Club had passed a resolution in favour of open tennis in the 1950s, and the L.T.A. had been promoting the idea at the I.L.T.F. since 1960. With no allies she could depend on with sureness, Britain could only raise the matter year after year until sheer frustration forced the present decision. Sweden was virtually our only steady friend. 'Honesty, and damn the consequences' was the stirring slogan adopted by the English committee when it was obvious that international agreement for a change in the rules might *never* be achieved just sitting round a table. Action and leadership were what was needed.

Derek Penman, chairman of the Rules Committee, summed it all up at the annual meeting of the L.T.A. when he said: 'For too long we have been governed by a set of amateur rules which are quite unenforceable. We know that so-called amateur players bargain for payments grossly in excess of what they are entitled to, but without which they cannot live. We know that tournament committees connive at this, otherwise there would be no players at their tournaments. We feel that we owe it not only to ourselves but also to our players to release them from this humiliating and hypocritical situation, and to make it possible for them to earn openly and honestly the rewards to which their skills entitle them . . . We have tried peaceful means and failed. Now we feel we can no longer endure the present situation.'

It was fighting talk, and it was widely resented, particularly where national self-interest was involved, as it was in many cases. The Italians and other Latins of Europe and America (who had had double standards going for them for so long they had no need for new rules, and feared the 'competition' of professional promoters) demanded our expulsion; the Russians appealed to the L.T.A. not to spoil Wimbledon's prestigious image; the French spoke privately of ever-perfidious Albion; the Australians spat at the All-England Club and the L.T.A., roundly declaring that 'no Australian players would enter an open Wimbledon'. It was all a great noise, but it came from empty vessels. The militant march music went in one end of a tunnel, and when it came out the other end, the panic chorus line ran 'If we can't beat them, we'll have to join them'.

When the 'we are going it alone' ultimatum was announced to the I.L.T.F. and its Italian president, Giorgio de Stefani, by the L.T.A., it very properly punctured instantly the inflated egos of certain members of the international body; it proved, if proof were needed, that now as always, where Britain led in tennis, the rest of the world followed. 'Self-determination' became the new parrot cry of members. The I.L.T.F. was by-passed by other countries within weeks, and a number of open tennis tournaments were announced in defiance of the Federation's dictates. Of the lesser 'opens' quickly fixed for 1968, Britain appropriately staged the first at Bournemouth, in April, 1968, and it was a best-ever occasion, except that some of the professionals taking part played disappointingly. So was the French open (delightfully won by Rosewall rather than Laver) which soon followed, promoted by a new young liberal group that had taken over power in France.

The first Open Wimbledon was even greater than expectations, primed at Bournemouth and Paris. It will go down in the memories of many who were there as one of the outstanding sports events at which they could ever hope to be present. In some ways, it was the best fortnight in 90 years. At this time there were two professional groups – the National Tennis League (with Laver, Rosewall and Gonzales among its stars) and the Handsome Eight, already mentioned. The two groups have since merged and expanded under the title World Championship Tennis. For some of the greats of tennis who had never won Wimbledon, because of their professional status, the first open tournament came too late, alas. But *all* the top professionals and amateurs were meeting head-on for the first time and there were no fewer than six former world champions in the lists, all but one of whom would have been barred under the old system. Shock after shock wave rose from most of the tournament courts, as this or that favoured player (professional or amateur) crashed to shock defeat in the early rounds. The public was being given lots of 'kicks' from the very first day.

Everyone wanted to see Rod Laver. When he had abandoned the amateur circuit in 1962 it had been uniquely as champion of the world (Wimbledon singles title) and of Australia, France, Italy, Germany and America. Now the left-handed, red-haired Queenslander was back on the Centre Court after six years in the 'rough' of the pro circus. Most money was on Laver to win, the more so as it was his declared ambition to win the first great open.

Bad weather affected form (but not spectator interest) in the first few days and a railway go-slow caused some would-be queuers to watch the tournament on T.V. instead. But local and world interest were equally at the sharpest peak ever. The seeding was much criticised (particularly the relegation of the evergreen great Lew Hoad to number seven) but the sixteen names chosen (in deference to the finest entry list ever) included all the greats, and must have been extremely difficult to compile.

The super sixteen in order of seeding were Laver (Australia), Rosewall (Australia), Gimeno (Spain), Newcombe (Australia), Emerson (Australia), Santana (Spain), Hoad (Australia), Gonzales (U.S.), Ralston (U.S.), Buchholz (U.S.), Stolle (Australia), Okker (Netherlands), Ashe (U.S.), Drysdale (South Africa), Roche (Australia) and Pilic (Jugoslavia) . . . not one from Britain, needless to say.

In fact Hoad went out to Bob Hewitt in the third round and, to the deep regret of many lady spectators, 40-year-old Pancho Gonzales (the eighth seed), went out in the third also, to the unseeded Russian, Alex Metreveli . . . while the popular Jugoslav, Nikki Pilic (16 seeded) had gone down in four sets in the first round. The other seeds who failed to survive the third were Santana, Drysdale and Gimeno. Rosewall, alas, too old by a fraction, would go out in the fourth to Roche. The men were rapidly being separated from the boys and the old men.

By the quarter-finals all four players in Laver's half of the draw were seeds. He played Ralston and won in five sets, 4–6, 6–3, 6–1, 4–6, 6–2, while Ashe put out Okker in four sets. In the other half, unseeded Graebner and Moore were meeting, with the young American the victor over the young South African fairly easily in three sets; and, finally, 15-seed, Roche, was vanquishing 10-seed Buchholz by four sets, 3–6, 7–5, 6–4, 6–4. The last eight had shared two classes, with four full professionals and four 'amateurs' (including 'registered player' Tom Okker). Laver was the only one of the first eight seeds to survive.

The fascinating semi-finals maintained the proportion of two amateurs and two professionals, and there was added excitement in the fact that each semi featured an Australian versus an American. In the event, Laver won through to the final fairly easily, in beating Arthur Ashe, the coloured American amateur, by 7–5, 6–2, 6–4, while Tony Roche of Australia overcame Clark Graebner of the U.S.A. in four much more hard-fought sets, 9–7, 8–10, 6–4, 8–6. So the stage was set for 'the final of the century', between the two super-professional left-handers, Roche and Laver. In fact, it was much more one-sided than might have been expected. Laver paced his games and sets to perfection, stamping his authority all over the Centre Court. Never once did he look like letting the punters down. The score of 6–3, 6–4,

6–2 sums up the superiority of the day of the champion of champions, the master of the 'sixties. And red-haired Rod made it a phenomenal tennis year by taking the grand slam of championship singles titles – the English, French, Australian and American – the first man to do so since that other red-head of the courts, Donald Budge, in 1938.

The ladies' singles title in the first open year was appropriately taken by the new professional, Billie-Jean King, of America, who had won Wimbledon the previous two years as an amateur. Having put out her fellow-professional, England's Ann Jones, far from easily in a three set semi-final that is remembered with awe, she sailed through a fairly easy pro-amateur final against big Judy Tegart of Australia, by 9–7 and 7–5.

Indeed, of the five open events at the first open Wimbledon fortnight, all went to professionals except the mixed doubles, which were won by Ken Fletcher and Margaret Court (who were really professionals, too, in all but name).

Britain's other great women's hope – other than Ann Jones, that is – was the brilliant but mercurial Virginia Wade (seeded number five), who had prevailed at Wimbledon, almost alone, against the might of America a month before to win the Wightman Cup for Britain. Then, alas, Virginia Wade went out 6–4, 6–3, to an almost-unknown Swedish girl, Miss C. E. M. Sandberg, in the first round of the first open. Although winning Wimbledon was as much Miss Wade's desire as any girl's, there was to be a tremendous boost for the unpredictable English rose when she was to become, later in 1968, the first Englishwoman to win the U.S. singles title for 38 years (the last being Betty Nuthall, in 1930) in overcoming Billie-Jean King by 6–4, 6–2.

All in all, however, the British name that deserves to be best remembered in connection with 1968 is that of Herman David, the ex-Davis Cup player who had been chairman of the All-England Lawn Tennis and Croquet Club since 1959. He it was who, probably more than any single man, who had the guts to lead Britain into more enlightened non-shamateur days in the summer game that is played and enjoyed by more people than any other sport.

A certain amount of unease and suspicion was creeping into open tennis even before the second year of 'honesty' in the game was properly under way. The amateur authorities (in the shape

of the International Lawn Tennis Federation) and the professional promoters (represented still by the National Tennis
League and the World Championship Tennis organisations)
had shown that they could work together after a fashion, but trust
was none too strong on either side. Little progress towards amity,
or even detailed consultation between the two sides, was to be
made in 1969, as was to be the case in 1970, with the result that
the game as a whole would move forward very little until the
searing clashes and splits of the early 'seventies.

Wimbledon's second open in 1969 (and the 83rd tournament
since the All-England Club launched large-scale lawn tennis in
1877), started badly for other reasons. The first day was completely washed out by rain. But fortunately, from the Tuesday,
the remaining eleven playing days were beautifully warm and
pleasant, so that the rearranged schedules were presented without
hitches. Attendances were well up on 1968, and prize money
had reached the phenomenal total, for tennis, of £33,370, with
£3,000 for the men's champion, and just half that for the
women's . . . a point that was to bring talk of Women's Lib in
tennis nearly sixty years after the suffragettes had first attempted
to burn down the Centre Court stands. To be fair, women were
technically still far behind, with no top woman standing a chance
in singles against any top man, and with their 'pull' with the
crowds that much less.

That being said, the great event for Britain in 1969 nevertheless was that Ann Jones (now a professional) came good at
long last in the singles, and pulverised the holder to win the
most coveted championship before the most partisan crowd since
Angela Mortimer met Christine Truman in the final of 1961.
Regarded by many of her international colleagues as the most
underrated player in the world, Mrs Jones prevented, in sterling
fashion, Billie-Jean King taking four Wimbledon singles titles
in a row and did it to the tune of 3–6, 6–3, 6–2, after a splendid
semi-final, in which she had put down Margaret Court by 10–12,
6–3, 6–2. It was a great triumph for a great English fighter.

The 'pros' also dominated the prizes in the men's events, with
Rod Laver again apparently-invincible in the singles (in which
there was again the full quota of 16 seeds) and do-or-die exploits
from veteran Pancho Gonzales providing thrills enough and to
spare. Astonishingly, Rosewall had gone out to the unseeded

Bob Lutz (America) in the third round. Ray Moore and Bob Hewitt (both of South Africa) had even more surprisingly gone out at the first, but only these three seeds had lightened the list by the fourth round. The last eight male survivors in due course were Laver, Drysdale, Lutz, Ashe, Newcombe, Okker, Graebner and Roche.

Perhaps the finest quarter-final, and one of the best matches seen at Wimbledon for some time was a tremendous duel between Graebner and Roche, which ended with victory for Tony Roche only after a final set of 20 games, and with the scoreline reading 4–6, 4–6, 6–3, 6–4, 11–9. And the semi-final also produced a hum-dinger when Laver met the bespectacled Arthur Ashe (regarded by many as his logical successor) – a player who seemed able suddenly to raise his game above even his normal great heights, as Rosewall, Gonzales and Hoad had been able to do before him, in recent times. In this case, the scoreline with its bare figures does not explain the thrills that the game offered, Laver winning 2–6, 6–2, 9–7, 6–0.

The other semi-final was also an excellent one, with Newcombe and Roche fighting it out at great length for the honour of tackling their compatriot on the Centre Court, and this time Newcombe was the winner at 3–6, 6–1, 14–12 and 6–4. The final, by contrast to all this, was something of a disappointment, with the mighty Rod disposing of his fellow-Australian fairly methodically in four sets, by 6–4, 5–7, 6–4, 6–4.

But the match many people will remember from 1969 Wimbledon is the one in the first round between the veteran and the young trailblazer – between 41-year-old Pancho Gonzales (who had succeeded Jack Kramer as the world's top professional nearly 20 years before) and 25-year-old Charlie Passarell, the Puerto Rican who was doing tremendous things with the W.C.T. professionals. Their match, stretching over two days and lasting, in all, 5 hours 12 minutes, was one of the emotional experiences of the decade, resulting in Gonzales losing the first set (the longest ever played in singles at Wimbledon) by 22–24 . . . losing the second set (in fading light) by 1–6 . . . and still winning through with the fantastic scoreline of 22–24, 1–6, 16–14, 6–3, 11–9.

The 27-year-old Aussie, Margaret Court, had her turn to set the seal of her undoubted queenship of tennis in 1970 – when, as well as winning Wimbledon, she achieved the rare 'grand slam' of the four major world titles open to women (those of Australia, France, England and the U.S.A.). In so doing, she became only the second woman in the long history of lawn tennis to do so, the first having been the late great Maureen 'Little Mo' Connolly. Mrs Court had also put herself in a class of her own in this, her greatest year by bringing her total tally of championship wins in world events to 77 (far ahead of what any other player had ever achieved) made up of 30 singles, 23 doubles and 24 mixed-doubles, and including six triple championships. This was, by the way, her third Wimbledon singles title, and she took it from her great rival Billie-Jean King in one of the best finals ever seen on the Centre Court, with tough, aggressive, no-mercy play the order of the day, and with the final scores of 14–12 and 11–9 taking two-and-a-half hours to achieve.

Laver, fading by now, not surprisingly, but still the leading attraction in World Championship Tennis (now the only professional group) failed to repeat in 1970 his Wimbledon singles successes of 1968 and 1969 for the hat-trick. It was John Newcombe's greatest year when he won the singles at the third open Wimbledon as a 'pro'. This was great, as he had also been the last amateur to win the title, in 1967, and he had been runner-up to Laver in 1969. The opposing finalist on this occasion was the incomparable Kennie Rosewall, also playing in his third final (the first having been against Jaroslav Drobny as far back as 1954. It was a long match and a great one, which see-sawed for nearly three hours before Newcombe squeezed through by 5–7, 6–3, 6–3, 3–6, 6–1. It was, incidentally, the first men's singles final to go to five sets for 21 years. Laver had gone out 4–6, 6–4, 6–2, 6–1 in the fourth round to Britain's Roger Taylor, to give the home crowd one of its happiest moments for many years.

Nobody had heard the name Lamar Hunt very much before the start of the 1971 lawn tennis season, but by the end of it, even the uninvolved viewers who solely sampled a bit of Wimbledon on the box for the fun of the big occasion had heard and read his name. An alleged-millionaire, and the 38-year-old son of a Texan oil speculator, Hunt (with his family) had been the brains and the money behind the now multi-million dollar business of the 24-man professional tennis circus for some years, having bought out the so-called McCall Group and amalgamated it in the W.C.T. organisation which he already owned (and of which the executive director is Swansea-born ex-player, Mike Davies). Hunt, an ambitious 'sportsman' whose money backs teams in four other sports, viz. American football, baseball, basketball and soccer, is said to like to be on the winning side, and to hate to lose money. There were also some who said that he believed money could buy anything in sport. What he apparently wanted from Wimbledon now was 'a piece of the action' in the form of guarantees, or a pledged share of the takings.

Towards the end of 1970, Hunt had captured half-a-dozen more young amateur stars, and the feeling among the more old-fashioned of the members of the I.L.T.F. was that this was what they warned would happen; national associations would be robbed of their player-assets as soon as these looked like paying off in spectator-appeal. Soon after this, I.L.T.F. delegates were further infuriated by reports that some of the top stars in Hunt's mono-poly organisation were likely to withdraw from some I.L.T.F. open tournaments (in alleged breach of faith) because they were 'too rich and too tired' to take so much 'punishing travel'. The uneasy peace that had simmered since 1968 looked like bursting open in 1971 with a vengeance. France seemed likely to be affected by this notion rather than Wimbledon. As Roger Taylor put it, giving the inside story on the rumblings: 'We need to play at places like Wimbledon for prestige and personal thrills, but there is more and easier money available in the States.' This was precisely what the 'old guard' of tennis had warned would happen if open tournaments were permitted – the rich would get richer and the poor poorer. Taylor also suggested that sponsors should be admitted to Wimbledon to boost prizes.

Mike Davies did not help matters any by hinting, a few months before Wimbledon '71, that even the championships at Church Road might be cold-shouldered by the leading pro-fessionals because W.C.T. was not being paid a fee for the services of its players. His point of view was that although Wimbledon was a prestige event, the group could not be expected to subsidise the 'pros' to play there. There was talk of Grand Prix tournaments for the professionals only being run in direct competition with the I.L.T.F.'s 30 major events. 'In 1970,' he said, 'of the seventeen W.C.T. players who competed at Wimbledon, only John Newcombe reached his weekly guarantee in terms of money won. We lost on the other sixteen.'

How much of this talk was the bluff of big business, no one could assess in the anxious early months of 1971, but Wimbledon officials apparently stood firm and resolutely refused (as they had done since 1968) to pay anything other than prize money to anyone, including the 'pros', this despite the fact that the French championships had been boycotted in 1970 by the top professionals for sticking simularly to their guns.

Although the professionals were in a strong position because of their fantastic popularity with tennis fans, the All-England club had a lot to offer, too and knew it. The weeks went past and the shouting (which had done no harm in terms of publicity, whatever other harm it had caused) died down. Suddenly, it became clear that every big name in tennis *would* be at Wimbledon, whatever happened at other tournaments (and Paris was again to be less favoured). And it apparently became clear, too, that various compromise steps, however short, were being taken to ease the two sides (i.e. the L.T.A., based in England, and the W.T.C., based in Texas) slightly closer together.

First, Britain chose to include the tennis 'pros' in national official rankings. Roger Taylor, who had won £17,500 in prize money in 1971, was listed at No. 1, with England's two other 'pros', Mark Cox and Graham Stilwell, at No. 2 and No. 4. Top amateur Gerald Battrick was sandwiched among the leaders at No. 3. This was resented abroad as being a major move towards full recognition of the professionals. It was in fact another enlightened British 'first'.

Secondly, a shock announcement came, in March, 1971, that the total prize money at Wimbledon in June would be cut by £3,860 to £37,790. To sugar the pill, it was added that £12,680 would be allowed in travelling expenses (not allowed since the first open in 1968), with the expense money being paid direct to the organisation sponsoring the player or players. This was immediately seen as a sop to W.C.T., their expenses being deduced as a substitute for the appearance money they had already been refused. Also, some individual prizes were altered. The men's singles champion was to receive £3,750 (an increase of £750 on 1970) with the runner-up getting £2,250 instead of

£1,500; also the women's champion and runner-up were to receive increases of £300 and £250, to £1,800 and £1,000 respectively. Increased admission charges were also announced, and these would result in revenue going up by about £30,000, so that the better prizes and expenses would be covered many times over.

At about the same time, the I.L.F.T. underlined the fact that lawn tennis was becoming really big business throughout the world, in that prize money on the world's major lawn tennis circuits was to soar to more than $1\frac{1}{2}$ million pounds in the 1971 season. This was to include the I.L.T.F.'s series of 35 Grand Prix tournaments worth £500,000 and the W.T.C.'s 21 events worth £450,000 . . . plus sponsorship money at other events worth at least as much again. 'If this proves to be a workable arrangement this year,' said I.L.T.F. president, Ben Barnett, 'it will be much easier to schedule tournaments in 1972.' For W.C.T., its European director, John McDonald, was equally placating : 'We control the majority of the world's best men,' he said, 'and therefore no meaningful championship can be held without our co-operation. But we understand that it is necessary that an international body be retained, for a host of reasons, in the interests of us all.'

One misunderstanding that did not help matters along was that British officials were apparently of the opinion (or was it business bluff again?) that Hunt's W.C.T. had total control over their 32 players, which was not strictly true. What they did have was a contractual guarantee that their players would play in all 20 W.C.T. tournaments. Other than that, all Hunt and Davies were able to do was to make a pledge that the 32 'Texas rangers' would be free of W.C.T. commitments on the dates scheduled for the main tournaments of the I.L.T.F. Rich individual players were still free to please themselves over dates, such as Paris '71, that they did not want to play, and the W.C.T. could apparently do very little about it. It was all a matter of responsibility. It was felt that top stars were unlikely to forget how much they owed to the game, but on the other hand with travelling pressures increasing all the time, there was the danger that they would call off occasionally, anyway, in order to enjoy a few weeks of family life now and then, here and there.

Matters were further complicated in early June, 1971, a few

weeks before Wimbledon, when the major 'warming up' tournament at Bristol was washed out to the point of severe curtailment due to weeks of torrential rain (although the long-range weather forecast had promised an unusually good 'flaming June'). This disaster threw out completely the pre-Wimbledon blueprints of several top players who had expected to use the Wills event at Bristol for serious match practice. And Wimbledon singles champion, John Newcombe, fell heavily on the damp court three times before going out in the first round to Nikki Pilic and upset his plan to be at the peak of fitness at Church Road.

When the seeding lists for Wimbledon were announced in mid-June, gamesmanship was again thought to be seen to be present and was greeted with loud squeals from the professionals and their leaders. The reason was that the All-England Club committee had chosen to reduce to eight the number of seeds (which had stood at 16 since the first open). This limitation meant that the learing 'pro' players had less protection than before. But from the other point of view, it greatly increased the likelihood of a lively first week, with more upsets and tougher-fought matches generally; in this way it was expected that first-week attendances, which had been declining slightly, would be greatly boosted. Marty Riessen (not seeded) gave the 'pros' point of view when he said indignantly: 'This is another attack on the professionals . . . It is ridiculous to have only eight seeds, and ridiculous that Tom Okker is not seeded. He is playing really well and winning a lot of money . . .'

In fact, there were no particular surprises in either the men's list or the women's list. Laver was sensibly placed above the holder, Newcombe because, as Wimbledon referee, Mike Gibson put it: 'Of all the players we considered, Laver had won nearly 50 matches against them and lost only a handful.' The men's list, which included five contract professionals plus three 'independents', gave the following order of seeding (with 1970 positions in brackets): 1. R. Laver (Australia) (1); 2. J. D. Newcombe (Australia) (2); 3. K. Rosewall (Australia) (5); 4. S. R. Smith (U.S.) (7); 5. A. R. Ashe (U.S.) (3); 6. G. C. Richey (U.S.) (–); 7. I. Nastase (Rumania) (8); 8. E. C. Drysdale (South Africa) (12).

And the women's seeds (with the only 'newcomer', the young French champion, Evonne Goolagong) read: 1. Mrs B. M. Court

(Australia) (1); 2. Mrs L. W. King (U.S.) (2); 3. Miss E. F. Goolagong (Australia) (–); 4. Miss R. Casals (U.S.) (5); 5. Miss S. V. Wade (G.B.) (3); 6 Mrs K Gunter (U.S.) (–); 7. Miss F. Durr (France) (–); 8. Mrs H. Masthoff (Germany) (–).

Ladbrokes' odds on the Wimbledon tennis championships, 1971 at this stage were as follow: Men's singles – Evens Laver, 6–1 Newcombe, 10–1 Ashe, 10–1 Rosewall, 10–1 Smith, 16–1 Richey, 20–1 Roche, 25 bar. Women's singles – 4–6 Court, 3–1 King, 8–1 Goolagong, 14–1 Casals, 16–1 Wade, 20 bar. William Hill's put Rod Laver at 5–4, Newcombe 5–1, Ashe and Rosewall 8–1, Smith 10–1 and Richey 16–1, with 20–1 bar; women's odds with Hill's quoted Mrs Court at 2–1 on, Mrs King 4–1, Miss Goolagong 8–1, Miss Wade 10–1, and Rosemary Casals 12–1. Plainly the 1971 Wimbledon fortnight was still wide 'open', and there was money to be made by all with prophetic vision.

Strangely, the equivalent tennis dangers to jockeys backing either themselves or other riders (which are recognised and absolutely forbidden by the Jockey Club) have never been much heeded by the L.T.A., although there is, in fact, a rule which says, somewhat obtrusely, that 'players shall not play for a stake, a declared bet, or a wager . . .' Tennis stars are certainly not specifically banned from backing themselves or from backing opponents in decisive matches. Such betting has always gone on in lawn tennis, and 1971 was no exception, with fairly heavy money from participants being wagered with the few top bookies concerning themselves with the event. Most players, not in with a great chance, were putting fairly substantial sums on John Newcombe to win. Nor was the reigning champion an exception : 'I consider myself a fair bet, even at 5–1,' he said early in the tournament, 'and I will be having £20 to retain my title. I usually have a bet because it gives me that little more incentive and adds another interest.' Roger Taylor, at the same time, was staking about £50 in bets on Evonne Goolagong, John Newcombe and others, and said : 'I would go all out to win, whatever my bets. To win Wimbledon would mean so much more than to win even £10,000, say, in betting.'

There was also some wagering on the weather, and no wonder, for prospects were damp, to say the least. Two weeks of almost continuous rain before the event had meant that (apart from the casualties already mentioned) none of the leading competitors had had anything like the normal preparation on grass for this, the world's greatest tournament. Indeed, the build up, both physical and psychological had been by far the worst for over 30 years. This meant that there could easily be freak results and surprise endings.

Attempts to introduce a new-style ball at Wimbledon for the 1971 tournament failed. France (at her devalued event, bereft of the top names a few weeks before) had been using a new Swedish ball for the second year running, the durability of which was its attraction. It conformed to International Federation standards, but the fact that it was pressureless apparently slowed down the game, according to some players and critics. Anyway, after efforts by the manufacturers to persuade them to decide otherwise, the All-England Club decided to continue with the Barnsley-made Slazenger balls it had been using since 1902. It was simultaneously announced that British Slazenger had won the contract for Forest Hills for the first time, in competition with Spalding, Wilson and the 'would-be revolutionary' Swedes who had taken the French contract away from Barnsley (temporarily, it was thought in Yorkshire).

One change *had* been made at Wimbledon. This was, in effect, the first real concession to the changing pace of life for over 90 years – the introduction of a tie-break scoring system. This deemed that, when any set, except the last, reached eight games all, the set would be decided by a sudden-death single game over the best of twelve points. It was to be introduced experimentally to reduce long sets, and if it took some of the fun out of tennis, as it might do, it was to be scrapped again in the future.

There had been an even more serious matter to be dealt with behind the scenes which had taken up a lot of time just before the 1971 fortnight. This was a sudden, serious shortage of strawberries (without which no Wimbledon championship could possibly get off the ground) caused by the heavy rain. But emergency supplies were rustled up from here, there and everywhere, with the result that the usual quota of 7,500 portions a day were available as usual in the event.

There were also worries about the speed of the playing surface of 'the fastest court in the world' – the Centre Court, which had been too little played on before the fortnight began.

Local schools had been chosen to provide the ballboys (those superb chameleons of the courts), the traditional Dr Barnado arrangement having been abandoned, but Commander Charles Lane had already knocked the 80 volunteers into shape and had given them their final warning against so much as scratching their backsides while play was on (the more so with ubiquitous T.V. cameras watching).

In other respects, although Wimbledon, 1971, promised to be as exciting as ever (and the weather was now good, getting better) Britain's representation and home interest in the events had dropped to a low peak once more. At one stage, just before the fortnight, there had been only four British names among the 128 starters in the men's singles (although this had risen to 10 when some lesser foreigners had scratched at the last minute. And in the ladies' singles, Britain had the smallest representation in living memory – 17 out of 128. Granted Virginia Wade was among the seeds (and Roger Taylor might have done well but for a suspect back) but there were few prospects to excite the patriot as Wimbledon got under way – not even the re-appearance of the sentimentally-regarded Christine Truman-Janes.

The draw had decided that four of the highest-paid sportsmen in the world would have to play their talented confrères and be knocked-out summarily, having to be content with the £100 pick-up reserved for first-round failures. And with the ladies, there were even greater reasons for tantrums, with an additional 'inside' battle of jealousies and ideology going on between the Women's Lib faction (or Women's Lob, as they had been dubbed) headed by Billie-Jean King, Rosie Casals and Julie Heldman, and the 'independents' championed by Margaret Court, Virginia Wade and Evonne Goolagong.

In fact, the heat was on in this respect already, because tension and tempers had flared the week before Wimbledon, when players had exchanged bitter words. It was all good, clean bad sportsmanship, and in the event tempers seemed to calm a lot in the cool of Wimbledon, although, at one stage, one lady did have her opponent in tears when she beat her decisively . . . but they were tears of disappointment rather than of rage.

As always, umpires came under heavy fire from players, with

the first of them being told to get his eyes tested before the tournament was ten minutes old, and this was obviously something the committee would have to look at most seriously before the 'seventies were much older. It was being voiced more and more that the standard of umpiring at Wimbledon did not bear comparison to the importance of the event, but at 50 pence per day, plus expenses, who could wonder at this? Money was again the obvious key to better things in the future, and this rate was a remaining stain on the All-England Club's image as the most efficient and progressive tennis club in the world.

Emotions were running high, as the fortnight progressed, in favour of 36-year-old, leather-faced Kennie Rosewall, the slight, brilliant Australian who had become a tennis legend in his lifetime but who had never won Wimbledon (mainly because professionals had been barred during his finest years). He had let it be known beforehand that he thought 1971 must be his last chance (although not his last appearance) and the crowd had responded by following him everywhere in his early matches. Appropriately, he had been awarded the M.B.E. in the Birthday Honours' List. But after enduring and overcoming a fantastic four-hour battle against Cliff Richey, twelve years his junior, in the quarter-finals (a truly memorable match that had the vast crowd thrilling to every fine stroke) the 'great little master' went down, predictably tired, in the semi-final to the hard-hitting champion, John Newcombe. Sadly he said, afterwards: 'I've got to accept that you cannot go on giving away ten or twelve years in match after match against strong young stars. But I'll be back to try again. The support for me at Wimbledon has been very touching, and it kind of breaks me up when I think that I cannot give the supporters the win they most want to see . . .' In fact, the winning did not matter so much in Rosewall's case, as far as he crowds were concerned. They will always relish the immaculate stroking and the splendid mastery of the classic values of the game he almost uniquely possesses in an era in which muscle power, alas, is the winning rule rather than the exception. Honour was rightly given him on the day his dream was shattered. As always, the best lawn tennis club in the world made the perfect gesture. Almost before the dejected Rosewall had stepped off the Centre Court, he was greeted with full ceremonial by officials and told he was to be made an honorary member of the All-England Club – an honour normally reserved for overseas champions, but this time, so very rightly, given to one of the greats of all time in lawn tennis.

Other veterans, or 'yesterday's men', as they were being called, had briefly delighted the crowds with the stylish magic of their play – notably the two 43-year-olds, Gonzales and Sedgman, probably making their last appearances at the greatest club in the world – but they, too, were out.

A below-par Laver having gone down the second Monday of Wimbledon (and looking at last as if his 'Rocket' would never again be quite sufficient to power him to victory on the last day on the Centre Court) the final of the men's singles became a less than glittering but certainly thunderous battle of the heavy-weights. It had saits stars John Newcombe and Stan Smith, the handsome, dark-moustachioed Sundance Kid, and the equally good-looking blond Army Private, Second Class; and it took place in the form of a clash that had more the flavour of a tough prolonged duel in a Western movie than a great lawn tennis occasion.

In a five-setter (only the second in a Centre Court men's singles final) of unrelieved Big Game savagery, which was engrossing enough at the time but is unlikely to linger in detail in the memories of those who saw it, 27-year-old John Newcombe, of Australia, soldiered home by 6–3, 5–7, 2–6, 6–4 and 6–4, to give 6 ft. 4 in. Private Smith of America his marching orders and record his third Wimbledon championship in four finals.

Meanwhile, astonishing things were happening in the ladies' singles. After a somewhat dull sequence of rounds, everyone suddenly woke up to the fact that a fairy tale was reaching its climax years before it was expected to do so, and that a new queen-in-the-making was in court and looking like the greatest natural tennis star since Little Mo Connolly. She was, of course, Evonne Goolagong, only 19, the latest in the great Australian traditions of sports celebrities: the babe from the bush; the sheep-shearer's daughter in from hard times in the Outback . . . and half-Aborigine, to boot, as well as being 'a real beut' in the language known as 'Strine'. Unbelievably, in view of her coach's pre-Wimbledon forecast that 'Evonne should be ready to win the Wimbledon title in 1974 . . .' she was through to the

final and facing the Grand Slam Queen, herself, Margaret Court
(having given Billie-Jean King a hiding along the way to make
her miss the final for the first time in six years.

Best of all, Miss Goolagong, flashing occasional half-smiles, as
though offering a taste of honey, showed that she had the best
kind of big match temperament when, unhurried and unflurried,
she rose serenely to the occasion to dazzle a rapt 14,000 Centre
Court crowd (some of whom had paid £25 for £5 tickets) with
an exhibition of graceful, intelligent and, at the same time,
aggressively killing strokes. To the delighted astonishment of
everyone present, she completely outplayed the world's best
woman player, Margaret Court (nine years her senior) to become Wimbledon champion in 61 minutes, by 6–4, 6–1. Big
Marg had no excuses (although she was to reveal later that she
was already pregnant at the time). She said 'Evonne plays better
when she has nothing to lose, and she is improving all the time.
I welcome an Australian taking my place.' If anything had under-
scored the fantastic changes due to take place in lawn tennis in
the 'seventies, it was the 'stealing' of the Plate (at only her
second attempt) by this teenage powerhouse . . . the first of what
was undoubtedly to be a record sequence of triumphs.

Indeed, Wimbledon, 1971, saw the end of a tennis era. The
old guard were routed on the courts, as they had been so recently
in international committee rooms. The courts, and the whole
ambiance of Church Road remained as great as ever, but a whole
new 'school' of players was sweeping away any traditional cob-
webs that may have remained from less go-ahead times. New
names were crying out to be taken to heart, in addition to those
that had thrust through to Wimbledon success. Chief of these
was that of Chris Evert, a 16-year-old American 'supergirl' who
was threatening (having had an unbeaten run of 47 matches in
the States, some of them against world-class stars) to make the
1972 Wimbledon a youth festival, as it had never been before.

Britain, still somewhat in the doldrums, had her prospects at
least for the mid-seventies. In September, 1971, a 17-year-old
Chiswick student, Glynis Coles, achieved one of the most remarkable feats in British tennis. In winning the Green Shield
British Junior Championship at Wimbledon, she accomplished a
clean sweep of a full quartet of national junior championships
for the year, and was rated one of the greatest home prospects

ever. Other British talent-in-the-making included the more-familiar names of Stephen Warboys, 'Buster' Mottram and Stanley Matthews; not forgetting Linda Mottram, Susan Minford, Ross Walker, Jill Cooper, John de Mendoza and Michael Collins.

Inevitably, however, all was not sweet promise for the All-England Club as preparations were made for the 1972 fortnight at Wimbledon. War had broken out again in July, 1971, between Lamar Hunt and Herman David (respresenting the 'pros' and the club respectively) and was to rumble on over the autumn and winter before another major confrontation would be needed in the spring to call the bluffs for another 'open' season. This time the signs and sounds were even more ominous. It had begun with a post-fortnight demand from Hunt for Wimbledon (which he acknowledged to be the best tournament in the world) to be improved, modernised, and turned into a much richer financial success ... to the mutual reward of the club and of his organisation which was supplying the stars-of-stars (this last point now being in some dispute thanks to the sudden surge of young talent to the fore). Fascinated by Church Road's garden-party air and fantastic audiences (on television as well as in the flesh) he wanted now to move in, take over the catering, sell advertising to the highest bidders, have manufacturers' display stalls, as in the States, and squeeze the world's television companies for more money. It was, of course unthinkable to Herman and his successful merry men at the All-England Club.

Other 'unacceptable' demands said to have been made direct to the International Federation are believed to have included a 'promotional payment' of between £16,660 and £20,000 annually by Wimbledon and by each of the other two major tournaments (France and America); ten per cent of all television fees; ten per cent of the amount by which the total income of the championships exceeded the 1971 level of income; the right to decide which manufacturer's tennis balls are used; the right to discuss what scoring system is most suitable; and agreement that 11 of W.C.T.'s 33 remaining tournaments to be for 'pros' only, 11 to be open and run jointly, with 11 open and organised by Federation member nations.

A meeting, called at Stresa, Italy, of the International Federation, then got tough as well as cross (several of its member countries, including the powerful U.S.L.T.A., having been snubbed by leading professionals, in alleged breach of good faith). It issued a proposal, amounting really to a lock-out, to ban all Hunt's men from playing at any tournament (including Wimbledon, of course) or at any affiliated club or court, from 1 January, 1972. Herman David and the L.T.A. were completely behind this move, flatly refusing to contemplate the professionals' further involvement in their tournaments.

The 'pros' were obviously worried, but it was very much in their interests to stand by their boss who was making them all richer than they could have dreamed of before he came on the scene. Wimbledon champion, John Newcombe, made a 'we-love-Lamar' speech. Rod Laver made a bid to sway the I.L.T.F. and failed. It was an apparent impasse and, later in the year, the silence became deafening.

This was, in the words of *The Times*, 'the end of a memorable era in the history of Wimbledon'. Appropriately, for a time of change and rebirth, it was coming up fifty years at Church Road and 100 years at Wimbledon's two venues for the All-England Tennis and Croquet Club. Rod Laver, Ken Rosewall, Margaret Court, and Billie-Jean King, who between them had graced singles' finals 20 times, had all gone down in straight sets in 1971 and were moving towards the outer courts of the lawn tennis circuses. The new young thoroughbreds of the 'seventies, from Australia, America and (it was fervently hoped) Britain were about to take over and compete for the favours of the discerning Wimbledon crowds, among whom schoolgirls and women were increasing in numbers every year, 'to see young golden men of tennis sweating it out for thousands of pounds,' as Fred Stolle thoughtfully put it.

Lawn tennis had been spawned at Wimbledon in the eighteen-seventies; it had grown gently and somewhat sleepily out of the leisurely vicarage game of croquet; and it had come of age, tentatively hand-reared amid fine froths of parasoles, multi-petticoats, social chit-chat and cream teas. The All-England Club had produced, over the century of its existence, a wealth of experience and a gift for improvement through gentle compromise rather than through commercial go-getting. It was unthinkable that all this tradition, comparable only to the Derby and the Grand Naional in its sense of sporting occasion, should be diluted by naked money-making processes. But it was now certain to be diluted, in 1972 at least. However, whatever the future held in the way of lock-outs, strikes, or disagreements, no one was in any doubt that Wimbledon would still go into its second century as *the* sporting showpiece of lawn tennis (the most popular of all world sports) and *the* tournament every young player would want to win and win again.

Index